D0362645

The Gardner Museum Café
COOKBOOK

Satyr and maenad gathering grapes, detail of a third-century Roman sarcophagus. West Cloister.

The Gardner Museum Café COOKBOOK

LOIS McKITCHEN CONROY
Foreword by Rollin Hadley

THE HARVARD COMMON PRESS
Harvard and Boston, Massachusetts

The Harvard Common Press
535 Albany Street
Boston, Massachusetts 02118

Copyright © 1985 by The Harvard Common Press, Inc.

All rights reserved. No part of this publication may be reproduced or
transmitted in any form or by any means, electronic or mechanical, including
photocopy, recording, or any information storage or retrieval system, without
permission in writing from the publisher.

Printed in the United States of America

Library of Congress Cataloging-in-Publication Data

Conroy, Lois McKitchen.
  The Gardner Museum Café cookbook.

  Includes index.
  1. Cookery. 2. Isabella Stewart Gardner Museum.
I. Isabella Stewart Gardner Museum. II. Title.
TX715.C5785 1985   641.5′09744′61   85-16803
ISBN 0-916782-71-9

All photographs courtesy of the Isabella Stewart Gardner Museum
Cover and interior design by Linda Ziedrich

10 9 8 7 6 5 4 3

CONTENTS

Soups

Quiches and Luncheon Pies

Main Dishes, Hot and Cold

Side Dishes and Salads

ILLUSTRATIONS

A NOTE
ON ISABELLA STEWART GARDNER
AND HER MUSEUM

Isabella Stewart Gardner was born in New York City on April 14, 1840. Her first connection with Boston came through a visit to Paris, where a friendship with her schoolmate Julia led five years later to marriage with Julia's elder brother, John Lowell Gardner, in 1860. The young couple established themselves in Boston, where Mrs. Gardner's independence of manner and thought excited a good deal of comment.

After the death of her two-year-old son in 1865, she endured several years of depression and illness. At a doctor's suggestion Mr. Gardner took his wife to Europe, her condition so poor that she had to be carried aboard ship on a mattress. Within a few months, however, she returned home in health and good spirits.

Mr. and Mrs. Gardner went abroad again in 1874, and afterward with increasing frequency. In a small way Mrs. Gardner had begun to acquire minor works of art, without thought of forming a collection, but in 1885, in Venice, she began to feel the power of the great masters of the Italian Renaissance. In 1888, in Seville, she bought her first old master, a Madonna by Francisco de Zurbarán (now catalogued as from his studio). At an irregular but accelerating pace, especially after she received her father's inheritance in 1891, she deliberately became a collector of fine art.

Like many fashionable Bostonians, Mrs. Gardner attended some of the lectures of famous Harvard teachers, and it was perhaps in Charles Eliot Norton's art history class that she met the charming and brilliant Bernard Berenson. After Berenson's graduation in 1887 she was one of those who helped him go abroad, where he soon became recognized as a leading connoisseur of art. From 1894 onward Mrs. Gardner relied heavily on his assistance in acquiring important works.

Two traits that help to reveal Mrs. Gardner's character were her love of music and her perceptive and amiable patronage of talent of every sort. Conductors, composers, players, singers, painters, sculptors, writers, and scholars were all the beneficiaries of her wealth of spirit and money. In a variety of quiet but effective ways she furthered many careers.

In 1898 Mr. Gardner died, leaving his wife in full control of his fortune. His death seems to have shocked her into an awareness that she, at fifty-eight, was no longer young, and she began furiously to work toward the realization of the museum that she and her husband had planned. A few weeks after the funeral she bought land in the Boston Fens, and while the foundation piles were being driven she left for Europe to look for columns, capitals, arches, ironwork, fireplaces, staircases, fountains, and other architectural elements that she wished to incorporate into the building. At the same time she continued to add to her collection of artistic masterpieces.

Mrs. Gardner returned home in December 1899 to supervise construction. She modified the plan often without a moment's notice, and required her specific approval of every detail. Her predilection was for the Italian Renaissance, and her vision of a museum was a Venetian palace of the fifteenth century, with galleries opening onto a flowering court. The dream became reality, planned in complete detail by Mrs. Gardner and erected under her constant and sometimes whimsical supervision. Before the architectural drawings were finished she had already decided where each imported pillar, doorway, arch, stone carving, or other structural member would be placed.

The seal that Mrs. Gardner designed for her museum was characteristic: a shield bearing a phoenix, symbol of immortality, and the frank motto *C'est mon plaisir* ("it is my pleasure"). It was part of her pleasure to keep her plans for the museum wholly to herself. Neither the architect nor the contractor was permitted to give any hint, and the Italian workmen, imported especially for the project, could not speak English. The effect, of course, was to whet public curiosity.

By Christmas of 1901 the building was essentially finished, some of the sculpture was in place, and plants were growing in the Court. The climax came on New Year's night 1903, the official opening. Mrs. Gardner's guests listened to a concert played by fifty members of the Boston Symphony Orchestra in a two-story concert hall, the upper half of which is now the Tapestry Room. Then the Court doors were opened, and the guests were admitted to a spectacle that was strange indeed in midwinter Boston—the balconies were hung with flame-colored lanterns, numberless candles flickered beyond the archways and windows, there were fragrance and color from the masses of flowering plants, and faint music came from the splashing fountains.

The first public opening was a few weeks later, on February 23, 1903, and from then on Fenway Court was periodically opened to the public. Mrs. Gardner lived in her great house quietly, giving only an occasional large party, but she enjoyed entertaining the distinguished friends she had acquired over the years. She continued to buy works of art and to arrange the collection in a distinctive, informal manner. She died on July 17, 1924, and was buried in Mount Auburn Cemetery, Cambridge, between her husband and her son. Her true memorial is the museum. Her will instructed that Fenway Court be maintained in its original arrangement "for the education and enjoyment of the public forever."

Today some visitors take greatest pleasure from the whole appearance of Mrs. Gardner's museum, the relation of the works of art to their setting and to the colors and the fragrances of the flowering Court. Together, these make up her composition, an embodiment of the concept of a grand house where people might have lived for generations surrounded by things that they cherished.

For information about visiting the Museum or becoming a member, write in care of 2 Palace Road, Boston, Massachusetts 02115, or call (617) 566-1401.

FOREWORD

The cookbook published under the Museum's name is, in reality, a personal compilation by the manager of our café. Lois McKitchen Conroy has built a solid reputation for appetizing and imaginative fare, prepared with limited time and space; her present work space was modestly conceived as a soup and sandwich shop until she demonstrated how much more could be achieved. In the belief that our loyal patrons and many others would like to share her secrets, the Museum has been pleased to encourage her in the production of this book.

It would be charming and of historical interest to know more about Mrs. Gardner's table. Several menus do exist, but the names of dishes without explanation leave too little to comment on, except that European travel had clearly had its effect. Isabella and Jack were known for their dinners long before they began renting the Palazzo Barbaro in Venice with its staff of twelve. They were accomplished hosts, used to discriminating guests. I imagine a table graced with English china and silver, a carefully chosen menu and sparkling conversation, and friends who went away refreshed, anxious to return another day.

In the spirit of those days, the Museum presents this cookbook to you. Buon appetito!

ROLLIN HADLEY
Director
Isabella Stewart Gardner Museum

PREFACE

When I started cooking at the Gardner Museum Café in 1982, we had one convection oven, one electric frying pan, and two soup warmers. At about the same time we switched from cafeteria service to table service, and wanted a set menu. These recipes reflect my efforts to produce a varied, substantial, and interesting menu with limited equipment and space.

The Café already served salads, sandwiches, hot soups, and occasionally quiche. (For lack of space, desserts were and still are bought from local bakers; for this reason no dessert recipes are included here). I made quiche available everyday—it was easy and hearty, and the fillings could vary. It could also be cooked ahead of time and reheated. This gave me the idea to try some of my family's recipes for pies. My French Canadian grandmother made Tourtiére (pork pie), which was traditionally served on New Year's Day in my family, and Salmon Pie. Both pies were a success in the Café; not only did customers love them, but they were easy to make. I began experimenting with some other family recipes, and adapting some old standards like Chicken Pie and Steak and Kidney Pie. With a salad or another side dish, they make a very substantial meal.

Soups were the most fun. It was almost impossible to make them from recipes, because none called for using an electric frying pan. So I started inventing soups, and making my own versions of classic recipes. I tried using unusual combinations of flavors, like tomato and ginger (Tomato Soup with Corn and Ginger) or tarragon and Worcestershire sauce (Corn Chowder with Tarragon), and found ways to make hearty, flavorful soups from everyday ingredients. I also found some pleasant ways to extend soups—necessary because we could make so little at a time. My favorite solution is the straight peach brandy called for in the Chilled Peach Soup with Watermelon Purée.

Each day we serve one special dish. In the winter it might be a casserole, a stew, or any main dish that can be cooked ahead of time. In the summer elaborate salads are very popular. I knew the Café couldn't produce a classic, perfectly grilled steak, or even a proper omelette, given our equipment. Instead, I tried to concentrate on combining fresh seasonal ingredients with flavorful spices, herbs, and sauces. We recently found a supply of local smoked seafoods. Experimenting with their products led to a new pie recipe (Smoked Scallop Pie) and to some hearty seafood and pasta salads.

I enjoy cooking. Each one of these recipes was fun to develop, and to cook and serve. All of the dishes are simple to prepare and require only a minimal knowledge of cooking. Many are perfect for entertaining because they are attractive to the eye and can be made ahead of time, allowing for more time to spend with guests. All the recipes are meant to be experimented with and adapted to personal tastes. I hope that preparing and eating these dishes will be as pleasurable for you as it has been for me.

The Gardner Museum Café
COOKBOOK

The Coquelin brothers, popular French actors, about 1890. Gardner Museum archives.

Soups

STOCKS

Miniature from the Collection of Poems, *written about 1490 by the Persian poet Hafiz. Tapestry Room.*

Vegetable Stock

3 quarts

3 quarts water
2 cups chopped eggplant
4 carrots, diced
2 large white onions, diced
1 pound mushrooms, sliced

3 stalks celery
1 clove garlic, crushed
4 bay leaves
1 cup fresh parsley leaves
2 cups dry white wine

COMBINE all ingredients. Simmer over low heat for 2 hours, uncovered. Strain through a fine sieve. Discard the vegetables.

Fish Stock

2 quarts

2 pounds fish bones or heads   3 bay leaves
2 quarts water   ½ cup fresh parsley leaves
2 cups dry white wine

RINSE the fish pieces in cold water. Combine all ingredients in a large pan. Simmer 1 hour, uncovered. Strain through a fine sieve lined with at least 3 layers of cheesecloth.

Hexagonal Chinese rice bowl, eighteenth century. Yellow Room.

Chicken Stock

4 quarts

5 quarts water
3 pounds chicken pieces with
  bones, such as necks,
  wings, backs, thighs
1 pound chicken gizzards and
  hearts

4 cloves garlic, crushed
4 bay leaves
½ cup fresh parsley leaves
2 carrots, diced
2 large white onions, diced
2 cups dry white wine

RINSE the chicken pieces in cold water. Place all ingredients in a large pot. Boil for 20 minutes, skimming off scum as it rises to the top. Reduce the heat, and simmer for 3 hours, uncovered. Remove from the heat, and strain through a fine sieve lined with at least 3 layers of cheesecloth.

Chill overnight. Before using the stock, remove the layer of fat that will have formed on the top.

Beef Stock

3 quarts

1 oxtail
6 pounds beef and veal bones
2 large white onions,
  chopped

4 carrots, chopped
3 garlic cloves, crushed
4 bay leaves
1 cup fresh parsley leaves

RINSE the beef bones in cold water. Place all ingredients in a large pot. Boil for ½ hour, skimming off scum as it rises to the surface. Reduce the heat, and simmer for 2½ hours, uncovered. Strain through a fine sieve lined with at least 3 layers of cheesecloth.

Chill overnight. Before using the stock, remove the layer of fat that will have formed on top.

SOUPS AND CHOWDERS

Madame Gautreau Drinking a Toast *by John Singer Sargent, 1882. Blue Room.*

Vegetable Soup with Ham and Mushrooms

8 servings

1 stick (¼ pound) butter
4 large cloves garlic, minced
1 large onion, diced
1 cup minced fresh parsley
¼ cup minced fresh basil, or
   1 tablespoon dried
2 bay leaves
½ pound Virginia ham, cut
   into thin slices 1-inch
   square
1 quart Chicken Stock

2 large sweet red peppers,
   diced
1 pound small mushrooms,
   quartered
1 cup dry sherry
2 cups cooked white beans
2 cups corn kernels
1 cup heavy cream
1 teaspoon ground black
   pepper
Salt to taste

IN A large frying pan over low to medium heat, melt half the butter. Add the garlic and onion; sauté until the onion is clear. Add the parsley, basil, bay leaves, and ham. Sauté another 2 minutes.

Transfer the mixture to a large saucepan. Add the chicken stock, and let simmer uncovered over low heat for about 20 minutes.

In the meantime heat the remaining butter in the frying pan over low to medium heat. Add the peppers, and sauté about 5 minutes. Add the mushrooms, and sauté another 5 minutes. Add the sherry; allow the mixture to simmer about 10 minutes, until the alcohol dissipates.

Transfer the mushroom mixture to the saucepan containing the other ingredients. With the saucepan over low heat, add the beans, corn, and cream. Let the soup simmer about 10 more minutes. Add the salt and pepper, and adjust the seasonings.

Fresh Vegetable Soup
with Sun-dried Tomatoes

8 servings

1 quart Vegetable Stock
¼ cup tomato paste
1 cup dry white wine
2 bay leaves
1 tablespoon grated orange
   rind
6 tablespoons butter
1 large white onion, diced
6 cloves garlic, minced
Dash nutmeg
2 large green peppers, diced
¼ cup chopped fresh dill
1 pound small white
   mushrooms, quartered

1 cup dry sherry
4 each: small zucchini and
   summer squashes, cut into
   small wedges
½ pound (4 cups) spinach
   leaves
1½ cups sun-dried tomatoes
   (available in Italian
   groceries and gourmet
   shops) cut into strips
Salt and pepper to taste

IN A large saucepan combine the vegetable stock, tomato paste,
and white wine, and whisk until the tomato paste dissolves. Add
the bay leaves and orange rind. Simmer over low heat, uncovered,
about ½ hour.

In the meantime melt 2 tablespoons of the butter in a large
frying pan over low to medium heat. Sauté the onion and garlic
until the onion is soft and clear. Remove to a large mixing bowl,
and mix in the nutmeg.

In the same frying pan melt 2 more tablespoons of butter over
low to medium heat. Add the peppers and dill; sauté about 5
minutes, then add the mushrooms. Sauté 5 minutes more. Add
the sherry, and let simmer until the alcohol dissipates and the
vegetables are lightly but thoroughly cooked. Transfer to the
bowl containing the onion mixture.

In the same pan melt 2 more tablespoons of butter over low
to medium heat. Add the zucchini, squash, and spinach; sauté
the vegetables about 3 minutes, until they are just cooked—

tender, but not too soft. Transfer them to a small bowl with a slotted spoon. Keep them separate from the other vegetables.

In the same pan sauté the dried tomato pieces about 3 minutes. Remove them and add them to the onion mixture.

Add the onion mixture to the vegetable stock in the saucepan. Simmer over low heat about 15 minutes.

Just before serving, add the zucchini, squash, and spinach mixture. Allow the vegetables to heat about 5 minutes. Add salt and pepper. Serve immediately.

Gingered Tomato Soup with Corn and Spinach

6 to 8 servings

6 tablespoons butter
1 large white onion, chopped
2 cloves garlic, minced
5 bay leaves
1 2-inch piece of fresh ginger, peeled and cut into small cubes
½ cup chopped fresh parsley
1 stalk celery, diced
1 medium carrot, peeled, trimmed, and cut in small pieces
2 cups dry white wine

4 cups water
6 cups tomato purée
¼ cup tomato paste
2 cups Chicken Stock
10 ounces (3 cups) corn kernels
8 ounces (3 cups) spinach leaves
Tabasco to taste
1 teaspoon salt
Ground black pepper to taste
2 cups tomato juice (optional)

IN A frying pan over low to medium heat, melt 4 tablespoons of the butter. Sauté the onion until it is clear and soft, but not brown. Add the garlic and bay leaves; sauté another minute, until fragrant. Transfer all to a large pot.

Add the ginger, parsley, celery, carrot, and wine. Simmer uncovered over low heat for about 20 minutes, until the alcohol dissipates.

Add 2 cups of the water, the tomato purée, the tomato paste, and the stock. Stirring frequently, simmer gently over very low heat for about 45 minutes, uncovered, until the vegetables are soft and the mixture has thickened.

In the meantime heat the remaining 2 cups of water to boiling. Add the corn and spinach; reduce the heat and simmer for about 8 to 10 minutes. Remove from the heat. Drain.

Remove the tomato mixture from the heat. Let it cool for about 10 minutes, then taste it. If the ginger flavor is strong enough, remove the ginger pieces from the mixture; if not, leave some or all of them to be puréed with the soup. Remove the bay leaves and parsley stems; purée the mixture in a food processor, or in small batches in a blender. Strain through a fine sieve. Add the corn and spinach.

If the soup is too thick, thin it with tomato juice. Season to taste with Tabasco and fresh-ground black pepper. Reheat gently, and serve immediately.

VARIATION:
Though refreshing, hearty, and aromatic when served hot, this also makes a spicy, clean-tasting chilled soup. Substitute olive oil for the butter, and chill the finished soup in an ice and water bath for about an hour. The soup should be very light; if necessary, add more tomato juice to thin it.

Vegetable Barley Soup

8 large servings

2 quarts Vegetable Stock	¼ cup minced fresh parsley
1½ cups barley	1 pound small white
2 carrots, diced	mushrooms, quartered
1 stick (¼ pound) butter	2 cups sherry
4 large cloves garlic, minced	Salt and pepper to taste
1 large white onion, diced	(about 1 teaspoon each)
4 bay leaves	½ cup grated parmesan
2 stalks celery, diced	cheese

IN A large uncovered saucepan over low to medium heat, simmer the barley in the vegetable stock until the barley is tender, about 45 minutes. Add the carrots; keep on a low heat.

In the meantime heat 4 tablespoons butter in a large frying pan over low to medium heat. Sauté the onion, garlic, and bay leaves until the onion is clear and soft, but not brown. Add the bay leaves, celery, and parsley; sauté for about 5 minutes, until the celery is tender. Transfer to the pot containing the barley.

Melt the remaining butter in the frying pan. Add the mushrooms; sauté until they are lightly done; then add the sherry and simmer for about 15 minutes. Transfer to the saucepan containing the barley and stock.

Add salt and pepper, and simmer the soup for another ½ hour over low heat. Adjust the seasonings. Serve topped with parmesan cheese.

VARIATION:
Beef stock may be substituted for vegetable stock; it gives a heartier, richer flavor to the soup.

Tomato-Lentil Soup with Cinnamon

8 to 10 servings

2 quarts Chicken Stock, or
   Vegetable Stock
¼ cup tomato paste
1 cup tomato purée
2 cups lentils
1 stick (¼ pound) butter
1 large white onion, diced
4 large cloves garlic, minced
6 bay leaves
¼ cup minced fresh parsley

4 stalks celery, diced
4 carrots, diced
1 tablespoon cinnamon
1 teaspoon allspice
Dash cloves
Salt and pepper to taste
   (about 2 teaspoons each)
1 pound (4 cups) chopped
   spinach

IN A large pot heat 1½ quarts chicken stock over medium heat. Add the tomato paste, and whisk until smooth. Add the tomato purée and lentils. Reduce the heat to low, and simmer uncovered for 1½ to 2 hours, or until the lentils are tender.

Melt the butter in a large frying pan over low to medium heat. Add the onion, garlic, and bay leaves; sauté until the onion is clear and soft. Add the parsley and celery; sauté until the celery is softened. Add the carrots, the remaining chicken stock, the spices, and the salt and pepper. Simmer for about ½ hour, until the carrots are softened. Remove from the heat.

Add the contents of the frying pan to the pot containing the lentils. Simmer for ½ hour, then add the spinach and simmer for another ½ hour. If the soup becomes too thick, thin it with hot water or chicken stock. Adjust the seasonings.

This soup is better the day after it is made, when the flavors have had a chance to mingle.

Gazpacho

6 to 8 servings

1 cup water
1 cup dry white wine
3 bay leaves
2 stalks celery
4 large green peppers
4 large ripe garden tomatoes
　(preferably home grown)
1 small white onion
2 large cucumbers
6 large cloves garlic

¼ cup fresh parsley, packed
　tight
½ cup fresh basil leaves,
　packed tight
½ cup olive oil or vegetable
　oil
3 tablespoons red wine
　vinegar
2 cups tomato juice
Salt and pepper to taste

IN AN uncovered saucepan over medium heat, simmer the water, wine, bay leaves, and celery until the liquid is reduced by half. Remove from the heat; strain, and let cool.

Remove the seeds from the peppers; chop the peppers very fine. Transfer to a large mixing bowl.

To remove the skins from the tomatoes, scald them in boiling water for 1 minute, then drop them into ice water and peel off the skins. Slice the tomatoes in quarters, and squeeze out the seeds; rinse under cool water to remove any seeds that remain. Chop the tomatoes very fine and add them to the bowl containing the peppers.

Peel the onion and chop it fine; add it to the bowl. Peel the cucumbers, cut them in half, and scrape out the seeds. Chop them and add them to the bowl.

Purée the garlic, parsley, basil, and oil in a food processor or blender, and add to the bowl. (Or mince the garlic, parsley, and basil, moistening with some of the oil. Then add to the bowl with the remaining oil.)

Add the vinegar, the wine reduction, the salt and pepper, and the tomato juice to the bowl. Adjust the seasonings. Serve very cold, garnished with mint leaves.

VARIATION:
One-quarter cup of fresh mint or tarragon may be substituted for the basil.

Minestrone

6 to 8 servings

1 quart Beef Stock
½ cup tomato paste
2 cups tomato purée
2 cups dry red wine
1 tablespoon dried oregano
1 tablespoon dried basil
1 stick (¼ pound) butter
8 large cloves garlic, minced
1 large white onion, diced
6 bay leaves
½ cup minced fresh parsley
2 large peppers, diced
1 small, tender zucchini, diced

1 large carrot, diced
¼ pound (about 1 cup) green beans, trimmed and cut into 1-inch pieces
½ pound (2 cups) spinach leaves
1 cup corn kernels
1 cup cooked white beans
Salt and pepper to taste, about 2 teaspoons each
1 cup grated parmesan cheese
Very small dried pasta pieces, such as miniature macaroni

IN A large saucepan heat the beef stock over medium heat. Whisk in the tomato paste until smooth. Add the tomato purée, red wine, oregano, and basil. Reduce the heat and let simmer, uncovered.

In the meantime melt half the butter in a large frying pan over low to medium heat. Sauté the onion, garlic, bay leaves, and parsley until the onion is soft and clear, but not brown. Add the peppers, and sauté for another 5 minutes. Transfer to the saucepan containing the tomato mixture.

In the frying pan melt the remaining butter over low heat. Sauté the zucchini for 5 minutes. Transfer to the saucepan containing the other ingredients.

Add the carrots, green beans, and spinach. Simmer the mixture ½ hour.

Add the corn, the white beans, the salt and pepper, ½ cup of the parmesan, and the pasta. Simmer for about 45 minutes; be sure the pasta is tender. Serve with more grated cheese on top.

This soup is better the next day, after the flavors have mingled.

Mrs. Gardner and companions in Venice. Gardner Museum archives.

Onion Soup
with Apples, Cheese, and Croutons

8 servings

2 quarts Vegetable Stock
1 cup apple brandy
1 cup dry white wine
1 stalk celery
½ teaspoon grated orange rind
1 large tart apple, halved
1 stick (¼ pound) butter
4 large white onions, quartered and sliced

6 bay leaves
¼ cup minced fresh parsley
Pinch dried thyme
Salt to taste
8 slices french bread, 1-inch thick
2 cloves garlic, minced
1 cup grated swiss cheese

IN A large saucepan combine the vegetable stock, apple brandy, wine, celery, orange rind, and apple. Let simmer over low heat while you prepare the other ingredients.

Melt all but two tablespoons of the butter in a large frying pan over low to medium heat. Sauté the onions, bay leaves, parsley, and thyme until the onions are clear and soft, but not brown. Transfer to the pan containing the stock. Let simmer over low heat for 1 hour. Add salt to taste.

About 20 minutes before the soup is done, mash the garlic and the remaining butter together. Spread the mixture on both sides of the french bread slices, then toast the bread under the broiler, turning once. Set the croutons aside and keep them hot.

When the soup is done, remove the apple and celery pieces and ladle into crocks. Float one crouton in each bowl. Sprinkle cheese on top, and place the bowls under the broiler until the cheese melts, about 2 minutes. (If crocks or oven-proof bowls are not available, let the cheese melt into the hot soup.) Serve immediately.

VARIATION:
Beef Stock may be substituted for the Vegetable Stock for a richer, darker soup.

Tomato Soup with Orange and Dill

8 servings

1 stick (¼ pound) butter
1 large white onion, chopped fine
4 large cloves garlic, minced
4 bay leaves
6 cups Chicken Stock
6 cups tomato purée
2 cups dry white wine

1 tablespoon grated orange rind
1 cup minced fresh dill
1 tablespoon sugar
½ teaspoon ground cumin
Salt and pepper to taste
1 cup tomato juice (optional)

MELT the butter in a frying pan over low to medium heat. Sauté the onion, garlic, and bay leaves until the onion is soft and clear. Remove from the heat.

Heat the chicken stock in a large pot over low heat. Add the tomato paste; whisk until smooth. Add the onion, garlic, and bay leaves; stir in the tomato purée, wine, orange rind, dill, sugar, and cumin. Let simmer about 1 hour.

Add the salt and pepper, and adjust the seasonings. If a thinner soup is desired, add tomato juice or more chicken stock.

VARIATIONS:

For a smoother soup purée in a food processor or in small batches in a blender, or press through a food mill.

For a creamy soup add 1 cup heavy cream and ⅛ teaspoon baking soda (to keep the cream from curdling).

Omit the dill, orange rind, and cumin, and use instead 1 cup minced fresh basil (or ¼ cup dried). Serve with a sprinkling of freshly grated parmesan cheese.

Omit the dill and cumin, and add ¾ cup minced fresh tarragon (or 2 tablespoons dried).

Omit the dill, orange rind, and cumin, and use instead ½ cup minced fresh sage (or 1 tablespoon dried).

For a vegetarian soup substitute Vegetable Stock for the Chicken Stock, with any choice of herbs.

White Bean Soup with Ham and Spinach

8 servings

1 pound dried white beans
6 quarts Chicken Stock
1 fresh ham hock
1 tablespoon ground cloves
1 teaspoon ground allspice
1 teaspoon ground nutmeg
Pinch of dried oregano
1 stick (¼ pound) butter
1 large onion, diced
6 large cloves garlic, minced
¼ cup minced fresh parsley
6 bay leaves
2 stalks celery, diced
½ pound Virginia ham or
smoked shoulder, sliced
thin and cut into 1-inch
squares

2 large white potatoes,
peeled, quartered, and
sliced
1 large carrot, sliced in thin
rounds
1 pound spinach, washed,
with stems removed
2 cups heavy cream
Salt and pepper to taste,
about 1 teaspoon each

SOAK the beans overnight if possible.

In a large pan combine the beans, 5½ quarts of the chicken stock, the ham hock, the cloves, the allspice, the nutmeg, and the oregano. Simmer over low heat for 4 hours, or until the beans are very tender. Add water during cooking if the soup becomes too thick.

Melt the butter in a large frying pan over low to medium heat. Sauté the onion, garlic, parsley, bay leaves, celery, and ham until the onion is soft and clear. Add the potatoes, carrots, and remaining stock; simmer for about ½ hour, until the vegetables are tender. Remove from the heat, and transfer to the pan containing the beans.

Simmer the soup for ½ hour more. Remove the ham hock and bay leaves. Add the spinach leaves, cream, salt, and pepper. Cook for about 15 minutes more, until the spinach wilts. Serve very hot.

Split Pea and Ham Soup with Cloves

8 servings

1 pound split peas
3 quarts Chicken Stock
1 fresh ham hock
1 tablespoon ground cloves
1 teaspoon ground allspice
Dash ground cinnamon
Dash ground nutmeg
4 tablespoons butter
1 large onion, diced
6 cloves garlic, minced

4 bay leaves
½ pound smoked shoulder or
   Virginia ham, cut in 1-inch
   cubes
2 stalks celery, diced
2 large carrots, sliced in thin
   rounds
Salt and pepper to taste,
   about 1 teaspoon each

IN A large pan combine the peas, 2½ quarts of the chicken stock, the ham hock, the cloves, the allspice, the cinnamon, and the nutmeg. Simmer over low heat for ½ hour, or until the peas are soft. Add water during cooking if the soup becomes too thick.

In the meantime melt the butter in a large frying pan over low to medium heat. Sauté the onion, garlic, bay leaves, ham, and celery until the onion is clear and soft. Add the carrots, the remaining stock, and the salt and pepper. Simmer until the carrots are tender, then add to the pan containing the split peas. Simmer ½ hour more.

Remove the ham hock and bay leaves, and adjust the seasonings. Serve very hot.

This soup tastes better the next day.

Black Bean Soup

8 servings

1 pound dried black beans
5½ quarts water
1 cup tomato purée
4 tablespoons butter
1 large white onion, diced
3 tablespoons minced garlic
10 bay leaves
2 tablespoons minced
    jalapeño pepper

2 tablespoons minced fresh
    parsley
2 cups dry sherry
Salt and pepper to taste,
    about 2 teaspoons each
1 cup grated monterey jack
    cheese (optional)

IF POSSIBLE, soak the beans overnight.

Combine the beans and water in a large pan, and simmer 4 hours or until the beans are tender. Add the tomato purée, and continue to simmer over low heat while you finish the soup.

In a large frying pan over low to medium heat, melt the butter. Sauté the onion, garlic, and bay leaves until the onion is soft and clear. Add the jalapeño pepper and parsley; sauté for about 5 minutes. Add the sherry, and simmer for 15 minutes; then add the contents of the frying pan to the beans.

Season with salt and pepper. Let simmer ½ hour more.

Remove from the heat. Purée half the soup in a food processor, or in small batches in a blender. Return it to the pan with the rest of the soup; reheat if necessary. Adjust the seasonings. Serve very hot.

If desired, pour the soup into crocks, top with Monterey Jack, and place under the broiler for about 3 minutes, until the cheese starts to bubble.

Fish Chowder with Peppers

6 to 8 servings

2 sticks (½ pound) butter
1 large onion, roughly
  chopped
6 cloves garlic, minced
4 jalapeño peppers, seeded
  and roughly chopped
2 large sweet red peppers,
  seeded and roughly
  chopped
2 large green peppers
¼ cup minced fresh basil, or
  1 tablespoon dried
¼ cup minced fresh parsley
6 bay leaves
4 cups Fish Stock

1 cup dry white wine
1 teaspoon ground mace
3 large white potatoes, peeled
  and cut into 1-inch cubes
½ pound codfish fillets, cut
  into 1-inch cubes
¼ pound halibut fillets, cut
  into 1-inch cubes
½ pound sea scallops
1 cup heavy cream
6–8 medium shrimp
1 large sweet red pepper
6–8 sprigs parsley
Salt and pepper to taste

MELT 1 stick of butter in a large frying pan over low to medium heat. Sauté the onion, garlic, peppers, basil, parsley, and bay leaves until the onion is clear and soft. Transfer to a large stockpot.

Add the fish stock, white wine, mace, and potatoes. Simmer for 45 minutes over low to medium heat.

Melt 6 tablespoons butter in a clean frying pan over low to medium heat. Sauté the fish and scallops until they are opaque, then add the heavy cream and simmer 5 minutes. Add to the fish stock mixture. Simmer the soup over low heat for 10 minutes.

In the meantime melt the remaining 2 tablespoons butter in a small frying pan. Over low heat lightly sauté the shrimp and pepper rings until the shrimp are just done, about 4 minutes. Do not let them curl up tight.

Ladle the hot soup into bowls. Garnish with the shrimp, pepper rings, and parsley sprigs.

Scallop Chowder with Pasta

6 to 8 servings

1 stick (¼ pound) butter
1 large onion, diced
8 cloves garlic, minced
6 bay leaves
5 cups Fish Stock
1 cup white wine
1 cup tomato purée
¼ cup minced fresh parsley
¼ cup minced fresh basil, or
    1 teaspoon dried
1 tablespoon salt
1 teaspoon ground black
    pepper

3 tablespoons minced fresh
    oregano, or 1 tablespoon
    dried
½ teaspoon ground cumin
1½ pounds sea scallops
3 large red peppers, sliced
    thin lengthwise
1 cup heavy cream
1 cup cooked white beans
5 ounces small pieces fresh
    pasta, such as pennette or
    tubetti

MELT ½ stick butter in a large frying pan over low heat. Sauté the onion, garlic, and bay leaves until the onion is clear and soft. Transfer to a large stockpot.

Add the fish stock, wine tomato purée, parsley, basil, salt, pepper, oregano, and cumin.

Melt the remaining butter in a large frying pan over medium heat. Sauté the scallops and peppers until the scallops are opaque. Add to the stockpot.

Add the cream, beans, and pasta to the chowder. Simmer for 10 minutes, stirring to make sure the pasta doesn't stick. Ladle into large shallow bowls, and serve with large soup spoons and forks.

Red Pepper and Sherry Soup

8 servings

1 stick (¼ pound) butter	4 large yellow peppers, seeded and chopped
1 large white onion, diced	
6 large cloves garlic, minced	1 tablespoon minced jalapeño pepper
8 bay leaves	
10 large red peppers, seeded and chopped	2 cups corn kernels
	¼ cup minced fresh parsley
3 cups dry sherry	3 cups heavy cream
1 quart Chicken Stock	Ground black pepper
1 teaspoon salt	

MELT half the butter in a large frying pan over low to medium heat. Sauté the onion, garlic, and bay leaves until the onion is clear and soft. Add the red peppers, and sauté 5 minutes. Add 2 cups of the sherry; simmer 15 minutes. Transfer to a large saucepan.

Add the chicken stock and salt, and simmer over low heat ½ hour. Remove from the heat.

In the meantime melt the remaining butter in a frying pan over low to medium heat. Add the yellow peppers, jalapeño pepper, corn, and parsley. Sauté 5 minutes. Add the remaining sherry, and simmer 15 minutes. Remove from heat.

Remove the bay leaves from the red pepper mixture. Purée in a food processor, or in small batches in a blender. Strain through a fine sieve. Return to the saucepan over low heat.

Purée the yellow pepper mixture the same way (making sure the processor or blender jar is clean first), but don't strain the mixture. Add the heavy cream, and place in a small pan over low heat.

Ladle the red pepper mixture into wide shallow bowls. Gently pour the yellow pepper mixture down the edge of each bowl, and swirl it into the red mixture with a knife, being careful not to blend the two. Top with fresh ground black pepper.

VARIATION:

This soup is also very good cold. Substitute vegetable oil for the butter. You might also add 3 tablespoons minced fresh basil to the yellow pepper mixture before puréeing.

Chinese porcelain lotus cup and saucer with famille rose *enamel. Yellow Room.*

Corn Chowder with Tarragon

6 to 8 servings

4 tablespoons butter
1 medium white onion,
   roughly chopped
1 large green pepper, diced
1 large sweet red pepper,
   diced
2 cloves garlic, minced
2 stalks celery, diced
4 bay leaves
¼ cup Worcestershire sauce
3 tablespoons dried tarragon

2 teaspoons salt
1 teaspoon ground nutmeg
1 teaspoon ground cloves
Dash paprika
4 medium red potatoes, cut
   in 1-inch cubes
3 cups water
1 pound (4 cups) corn
   kernels
1 quart heavy cream
Ground black pepper

MELT the butter in a frying pan over low to medium heat. Sauté the onion, peppers, garlic, and celery until soft and clear, but not brown. Add the bay leaves and sauté for another minute, until fragrant.

Add the Worcestershire sauce, tarragon, salt, spices, potatoes, and water. Let simmer uncovered 40 minutes, until the liquid reduces to about 2 cups. Add the corn.

Transfer the mixture to a large pot; add the heavy cream. Heat and simmer gently for 20 minutes.

Ladle the chowder into bowls, and top with a dash of fresh-ground pepper.

This makes a wonderful main dish for 6 when served with Mandarin Orange, Walnut, and Papaya Salad and warm crusty pumpernickel bread with butter. Or serve it as an appetizer for 8 with a light main dish.

Spiced Pear and Celery Soup

6 to 8 servings

1 stick (¼ pound) butter
1 large white onion, chopped fine
1 teaspoon minced garlic
2 bay leaves
2½ cups Chicken Stock
¼ cup minced cilantro (also called chinese parsley or coriander)
1 tablespoon ground nutmeg
2 tablespoons peeled and grated gingerroot
1 tablespoon celery seed
1 teaspoon salt
1 teaspoon ground white pepper
½ cup dry sherry
4 stalks celery, trimmed to 8-inch lengths and sliced
5 anjou pears, peeled, cored, and sliced lengthwise
1 cup heavy cream
1 tablespoon grated orange rind

IN A large frying pan over low to medium heat, melt half the butter. Sauté the onion, garlic, and bay leaves until the onion is soft and clear. Transfer to a large stockpot. Add the chicken stock, cilantro, nutmeg, ginger, celery seed, salt, pepper, and sherry. Bring to a boil; reduce the heat and let simmer.

In the meantime melt the remaining butter in the frying pan. Sauté the celery over low heat until softened. Add the pears; sauté for about 5 minutes. Transfer the mixture to the stockpot containing the chicken stock mixture.

Let the soup simmer uncovered for 1 hour, then stir in the cream and the orange rind. Purée in a food processor, or in small batches in a blender, until smooth. Adjust the seasonings; serve hot.

Chilled Strawberry and Melon Soup

6 to 8 servings

3 pints strawberries, hulled
and sliced lengthwise
3 cups dry white wine
½ teaspoon peeled and
grated gingerroot
1 teaspoon ground nutmeg
½ cup dry sherry

1 large cantaloupe
1 honeydew melon
1 tablespoon minced fresh
mint, and 16 well-shaped
leaves
½ cup blueberries, firm and
well shaped

IN AN uncovered saucepan over low heat, simmer 2 pints of
the strawberries, the white wine, the ginger, and the nutmeg for
about ½ hour, until the alcohol dissipates. Remove from the
heat; transfer to a bowl and set aside to cool.

In the meantime place the remaining strawberries and the
sherry in another large bowl. Remove the rind and seeds from
both melons. Cut the melons in half, and cut one half of each
in half again. Chop the quarters into very tiny pieces, saving the
juice with the flesh. Add this to the strawberry and sherry mixture.

Roughly chop the remaining melon halves, saving the juice.
Add to the cooked strawberry and wine mixture. Add the
chopped mint (reserve the whole leaves). Purée the mixture in
a food processor, or in small batches in a blender, until smooth.

Add the purée to the bowl containing the strawberries, sherry,
and chopped melon. Mix well. Let sit in the refrigerator for 1
hour to allow the flavors to mix. The soup should be served well
chilled; refrigerate longer if necessary.

Serve in chilled bowls, garnished with blueberries arranged in
clusters and whole mint leaves.

Chilled Peach Soup with Watermelon Purée

6 to 8 servings

6 large ripe peaches, peeled, pitted, and sliced
1 1-inch piece of gingerroot, peeled
1 teaspoon ground nutmeg
½ teaspoon ground mace
1 teaspoon grated lemon rind
3 cups dry white wine
1 cup water
4 cups puréed or minced watermelon flesh
1 cup peach brandy
3 tablespoons chopped fresh mint
1 cup heavy cream (optional)

IN A large, uncovered Teflon-coated or noncorrodible saucepan, simmer the peaches, ginger, nutmeg, mace, lemon rind, wine, and water over moderate heat. Let cook until the liquid is syrupy and the peaches and ginger are soft, about 45 minutes. Remove from the heat; let cool 1 hour.

Remove the ginger, and purée the mixture in a food processor or in small batches in a blender. Strain through a fine sieve.

Add the watermelon purée and the peach brandy. Ladle into bowls and garnish with chopped mint.

VARIATION:
Heavy cream may be added to produce a smoother, richer soup.

Chinese rice bowl with peaches and bats, eighteenth century. Yellow Room.

Chilled Nectarine Soup with Champagne

6 to 8 servings

1 cup orange juice
3 cups dry white wine
6 large ripe nectarines, peeled
and sliced thin
1 teaspoon ground mace
1 cantaloupe
6–8 large strawberries, hulled
and sliced

1 cup crème de cassis (black
currant liqueur)
4 cups very dry champagne
(brut)
¼ cup large blueberries, firm
and well shaped
6–8 mint leaves

IN A large, uncovered saucepan, simmer the orange juice, wine, nectarines, and mace for 45 minutes, or until the liquid is syrupy and the fruit is soft. Remove from the heat. Transfer to a large bowl, and chill.

Remove the rind and seeds from the cantaloupe. Chop it roughly and save the juice. Purée the flesh and juice in a food processor, or in small batches in a blender, till smooth. Add to the nectarine mixture.

Add the strawberries and cassis to the mixture. Let the soup sit in the refrigerator for 1 hour so the flavors can mix; refrigerate longer, if necessary, until the soup is well chilled.

Add the champagne just before serving. Ladle the soup into bowls, making sure the strawberries are evenly distributed. Garnish with the blueberries and mint leaves.

Gingered Cream of Carrot Soup

8 servings

1 stick (¼ pound) butter
1 large white onion, chopped
8 large cloves garlic, chopped
6 bay leaves
¼ cup chopped fresh parsley
2 cups dry white wine
1 pound carrots, sliced
1 quart Chicken Stock
2 tablespoons peeled and
   grated gingerroot
2 teaspoons curry powder

1 teaspoon ground cloves
1 teaspoon celery seed
Dash cinnamon
Dash nutmeg
Salt and pepper to taste,
   about 1 teaspoon each
1 quart heavy cream
1 tablespoon grated orange
   rind, soaked in 1
   tablespoon dry sherry

MELT the butter in a frying pan over low to medium heat. Sauté the onion, garlic, bay leaves, and parsley till the onion is clear and soft. Transfer to a large saucepan.

Add the wine, carrots, chicken stock, spices, and salt. Simmer over low heat for 1 hour, uncovered. The liquid should reduce by half.

Purée the soup in a food processor or blender. Strain it through a fine sieve, and return it to the pot.

Add the heavy cream and reheat. Adjust the seasonings. Serve very hot, garnished with a sprinkling of orange rind.

Chilled Cream of Tomato Soup

6 to 8 servings

¼ cup vegetable oil
1 large white onion, chopped
4 cloves garlic, minced
6 bay leaves
5 large ripe tomatoes
2 cups Vegetable Stock

⅛ teaspoon baking soda
¾ cup minced fresh basil
1 teaspoon salt
2 cups heavy cream
Ground black pepper

HEAT the oil in a large frying pan over medium heat. Sauté the onion, garlic, and bay leaves until the onion is soft and clear. Remove from the heat and set aside.

To peel the tomatoes, plunge them into boiling water for 3 minutes, then into ice water for 3 minutes. The skins should come off easily. Slice the tomatoes in half, squeeze out the seeds, and rinse to remove the remaining seeds. Chop the tomatoes roughly.

In a large stockpot combine the onion mixture, tomatoes, wine, vegetable stock, and baking soda. Bring to a boil; reduce the heat and simmer for 45 minutes, uncovered. Remove from the heat. Purée the mixture in a food processor or in small batches in a blender, or press through a food mill until the mixture is smooth. Strain through a fine sieve.

Add the basil, salt, and heavy cream. Let cool, then chill in the refrigerator for 1 hour. Ladle into bowls; garnish with fresh-ground black pepper.

Spinach and Potato Soup

6 to 8 servings

1 stick (¼ pound) butter
2 large white onions, diced
6 cloves garlic, minced
6 bay leaves
2 cups dry sherry
6 medium white potatoes,
   peeled and sliced thin
1 quart Chicken Stock

6 slices bacon, cut into 1-
   inch pieces
3 cups washed and trimmed
   spinach leaves, firmly
   packed
1 teaspoon salt
1 quart heavy cream
Ground black pepper

MELT the butter in a large frying pan over medium heat. Sauté the onions, garlic, and bay leaves until the onions are clear and soft. Transfer to a large pot.

Add the sherry, potatoes, and chicken stock. Bring to a boil; reduce the heat and let simmer uncovered for about 45 minutes. Purée in a food processor, or in small batches in a blender. Return to the pot.

Fry the bacon in the frying pan till crisp. Drain off most of the grease. Add the spinach, and sauté until it wilts. Add the bacon and spinach to the mixture in the pot.

Add the salt and cream. Simmer for 20 minutes. Adjust the seasonings. Serve garnished with pepper.

Cream of Broccoli Soup

6 to 8 servings

1 stick (¼ pound) butter
1 large onion, diced
6 cloves garlic, minced
6 bay leaves
1 large bunch (2 pounds)
   broccoli
2 tablespoons dried basil

1 tablespoon ground nutmeg
1 quart Chicken Stock
2 cups white wine
1 quart heavy cream
Salt and pepper to taste,
   about 1 teaspoon each

MELT half the butter in a large frying pan over low to medium heat. Sauté the onion, garlic, and bay leaves until the onion is clear and soft. Transfer to a large pot.

Separate the broccoli florets from the stems. Chop the florets and set aside. Trim 1 inch off the stems; chop the stems into small pieces. Add the stems to the pot containing the onion. Add the basil, nutmeg, chicken stock, and wine. Bring to a boil; reduce the heat and simmer uncovered for 45 minutes to 1 hour, or until the liquid reduces by about a third.

Remove the bay leaves. Purée the soup in a food processor, or in small batches in a blender, until smooth. Return to the pot.

Melt the remaining butter in a frying pan over low to medium heat. Sauté the broccoli florets for about 5 minutes; do not let them brown. Add the heavy cream and simmer for 5 minutes.

Add the florets and cream to the puréed broccoli in the pot. Add salt and pepper. Simmer 20 minutes. Adjust the seasonings, and serve.

Cream of Mushroom Soup

6 to 8 servings

1 stick (¼ pound) butter
2 large onions, diced
6 cloves garlic, minced
6 bay leaves
¼ cup minced fresh parsley
1 pound small white
    mushrooms, sliced

2 cups dry sherry
3 cups Chicken Stock
1 quart heavy cream
Salt and pepper to taste,
    about 1 teaspoon each

MELT the butter in a large frying pan over low to medium heat. Sauté the onions, garlic, bay leaves, and parsley until the onions are soft and clear. Add the mushrooms; sauté for about 5 minutes. Add the sherry; simmer 15 minutes. Transfer to a large stockpot.

Add the chicken stock. Simmer for 40 minutes uncovered; the liquid will reduce. Add the heavy cream, salt, and pepper. Simmer for 15 minutes. Adjust the seasonings and serve.

Chilled Cream of Cucumber Soup

6 to 8 servings

¼ cup vegetable oil
1 large white onion, chopped
2 cups dry white wine
2 cups Chicken Stock
1 teaspoon ground cumin
1 teaspoon ground mace

¾ cup chopped fresh dill
6 large cucumbers, peeled, seeded, and chopped
1 cup cold heavy cream
2 cups light cream
Salt and pepper to taste

HEAT the oil in a large frying pan over low to medium heat. Sauté the onion till it is clear and soft. Transfer to a large stockpot.

Add the wine, chicken stock, cumin, and mace. Simmer uncovered ½ hour.

Add the dill, and simmer for 2 minutes. Remove from the heat, and add the heavy cream immediately to stop the mixture from cooking further. Add the cucumbers.

Purée the mixture in a food processor, or in small batches in a blender. Transfer to a large serving bowl.

Add the light cream, salt, and pepper. Adjust the seasonings and serve.

Vegetable Tortellini

6 to 8 servings

1 stick plus 2 tablespoons
   butter
1 large white onion, diced
6 cloves garlic, minced
4 bay leaves
¼ cup minced fresh parsley
¼ cup minced fresh basil, or
   1 tablespoon dried
½ pound small white
   mushrooms, sliced
1 quart Beef Stock
3 cups dry red wine

1 tablespoon grated orange
   rind
1 tablespoon dried oregano
2 large carrots, diced
½ cup tomato paste
1 cup tomato purée
10 ounces fresh meat
   tortellini
2 small zucchini, quartered
   and sliced
Salt and pepper to taste

MELT 1 stick of butter in a large frying pan over low to medium heat. Sauté the onion, garlic, bay leaves, parsley, basil, and mushrooms till the onion is soft and clear. Transfer to a large stockpot.

Add the beef stock, wine, orange rind, oregano, carrots, tomato paste, and tomato purée. Bring to a boil; reduce the heat, and simmer uncovered for 40 minutes.

In the meantime bring the water to a boil in another pan. Add the tortellini and cook for 4 minutes. Drain and rinse well with cool water to keep the pasta from sticking together. Set aside.

Melt the remaining butter in a frying pan over low to medium heat. Sauté the zucchini till lightly cooked but still firm, about 4 minutes. Remove from the heat.

Add salt and pepper to the soup; adjust the seasonings. Divide the tortellini and zucchini among soup bowls. Ladle very hot soup over both. Allow 2 minutes for the soup to heat the tortellini through, then serve.

You see, merry Phillis, that dear little maid,
   Has invited Belinda to tea;
Her nice little garden is shaded by trees,—
   What pleasanter place could there be?

There's a cake full of plums, there are strawberries too,
   And the table is set on the green;
I'm fond of a carpet all daisies and grass,—
   Could a prettier picture be seen?

A blackbird (yes, blackbirds delight in warm weather,)
   Is flitting from yonder high spray;
He sees the two little ones talking together,—
   No wonder the blackbird is gay!

"Two Little Girls at Tea" from Under the Willow *by Kate Greenaway. Library.*

Chilled Plum Soup with Cassis

6 to 8 servings

12 tart red plums, pitted and
  sliced (do not peel)
4 cups dry white wine
1 1-inch piece peeled
  gingerroot

1 teaspoon ground nutmeg
1 cup water
4 cups cassis (black currant
  liqueur)
8 sprigs mint

IN A large, uncovered saucepan over low heat simmer the plums, wine, ginger, nutmeg, and water for 45 minutes, or until the liquid is syrupy and the fruit is soft.

Puree the mixture in a food processor, or in small batches in a blender. Strain through a fine sieve. Transfer to a serving bowl, add the cassis, and chill.

Serve garnished with mint sprigs.

Smoked Scallop Bisque

6 to 8 servings

4 tablespoons butter
1 large white onion, diced
4 cloves garlic, minced
1 medium sweet red pepper,
  seeded and chopped
4 bay leaves
1 pound smoked bay scallops
1 quart Fish Stock

2 cups dry vermouth
1 pound fresh sea scallops
1 teaspoon oregano
2 cups heavy cream
1 teaspoon salt
1 tablespoon ground white
  pepper

HEAT the butter in a frying pan over low to medium heat. Sauté the onion, garlic, red pepper, and bay leaves, until the onion is clear. Transfer to a large stockpot.

Add the smoked scallops, fish stock, vermouth, sea scallops, and oregano. Simmer uncovered over low heat for 1 hour; the liquid will reduce by half.

Purée the mixture in a food processor, or in small batches in a blender. Strain through a fine sieve.

Add the cream, salt, and pepper. Reheat in a clean stockpot. Let simmer for 15 minutes, then adjust the seasonings. If the soup is too thick, thin with additional heavy cream or fish stock.

This bisque is very rich. It is best served with mild crackers and followed by a light main dish, such as Shrimp and Beef Salad with Tropical Fruit or Chilled Baked Tomatoes Stuffed with Ratatouille and Pesto. For a less smoky taste alter the ratio of smoked to fresh scallops.

Cream of Zucchini Soup

6 to 8 servings

6 medium-sized, firm zucchini	2 medium sweet red peppers, seeded and sliced lengthwise
1 quart Chicken Stock	
¾ cup minced fresh basil, or 3 tablespoons dried	1 cup dry sherry
4 bay leaves	1 quart heavy cream
4 tablespoons butter	1 teaspoon salt
1 medium white onion, diced	1 tablespoon ground black pepper
4 cloves garlic, minced	

WASH and trim the zucchini, and roughly chop 3 of them. In a large uncovered saucepan over medium heat, simmer the chopped zucchini, chicken stock, basil and bay leaves for 1 hour, or until the liquid is reduced. Set aside.

Quarter and slice the remaining zucchini.

Heat the butter in a frying pan over low to medium heat. Sauté the onion, garlic, and red peppers until the onion is clear. Add the sherry and zucchini slices. Simmer uncovered over low heat for 20 minutes. Transfer to a large pot.

While the sherry mixture simmers, remove the bay leaves from the stock mixture. Purée the stock mixture in a food processor, or in small batches in a blender, until very smooth. Add to the mixture in the pot.

Add the cream, salt, and pepper. Simmer over low heat for 20 minutes. Adjust the seasonings, and serve.

Overleaf: the Museum's central court.

Quiches and Luncheon Pies

PIE CRUST

Veneto-Islamic brass plate, sixteenth century. Long Gallery.

Unbaked Pie Shell

For a 9-inch pie or quiche

1¼ cups all-purpose flour
1 teaspoon salt
⅓ cup cold vegetable
  shortening

2 tablespoons cold butter
5 tablespoons cold water

SIFT together the flour and salt into a large bowl.

With a pastry cutter or 2 knives, cut in the cold shortening and butter until pea-sized pieces form.

With a fork, mix in the water 1 tablespoon at a time, until large balls form.

Flour a pastry cloth and rolling pin. Roll out the dough until it is large enough to fit the pie plate or quiche pan with a 1-inch overhang. Line the pan, being careful not to handle the dough too much. Fold under the edges and crimp.

PASTRY FOR A DOUBLE-CRUST PIE

For a 9-inch pie

Double the preceding recipe, and divide the dough in half. Roll out the bottom crust with a ½-inch overhang. After adding the filling, roll out the top crust with a ½-inch overhang. Fold the edges under and crimp. Vent the top.

True quiche pans have 2-inch vertical sides that are fluted. You can make a quiche in a regular pie pan, but the shell must be tall and very firm to support the custard as it sets.

QUICHES

Mrs. Gardner's luncheon party during a fiesta in Seville, Spain, in 1888. Gardner Museum archives.

Potato Quiche
with Scallions and Cream Cheese

6 servings

6 small new potatoes (about
    3 inches long), sliced very
    thin
1 cup cream cheese, softened
2 tablespoons fresh dill
1½ cups light cream
2 tablespoons butter
6 large scallions, trimmed
    and chopped

6 eggs
1 teaspoon salt
1 teaspoon ground black
    pepper
½ cup grated sharp cheddar
    cheese
1 Unbaked Pie Shell

BOIL the potatoes until they are soft but still firm, about 5
minutes. Drain and set aside.

Combine the cream cheese, dill, and ¼ cup of the light cream
in a large mixing bowl. Beat on low speed with an electric mixer
for 3 minutes, until the dill is well distributed and the mixture
is creamy.

Heat the butter in a small frying pan over low to medium
heat. Sauté the scallions until they are softened but not brown,
about 5 minutes. Reduce the heat to very low. Add the cream
cheese, and allow it to melt, stirring constantly (about 3 to 5
minutes). Turn off the heat.

In a large mixing bowl combine the eggs, remaining cream,
salt, and pepper. Beat well with an electric mixer or by hand
with a wire whisk.

Spread the potatoes evenly over the bottom of the quiche shell.
Spread the cream cheese mixture over the potatoes, and sprinkle
the grated cheddar over the cream cheese. Pour in the egg mixture. With your fingers, gently mix the filling, being careful not
to damage the bottom of the pie shell.

Bake the quiche at 425° for 10 minutes, then reduce the heat
to 300°. Bake for 25 to 30 minutes, until a knife inserted in the
center comes out clean. If the top of the quiche becomes too
brown, cover it with a piece of buttered aluminum foil.

Spinach, Cheddar, and Pesto Quiche

6 servings

3 tablespoons butter
1 small white onion, diced
½ pound washed and
  trimmed spinach
6 eggs
1¼ cups light cream

1 teaspoon salt
1 teaspoon ground black
  pepper
1 cup grated sharp cheddar
  cheese
1 Unbaked Pie Shell

FOR THE PESTO:
2 cups washed fresh basil
  leaves
4 cloves garlic, minced
½ teaspoon salt
½ teaspoon pepper

¼ cup pine nuts
½ cup grated parmesan
  cheese
¼ cup olive oil

PURÉE the pesto ingredients in a food processor, or in small batches in a blender. Set aside in a mixing bowl.

Heat the butter in a frying pan over low heat. Sauté the onion until soft and clear. Add the spinach; sauté until the spinach is cooked and any liquid has evaporated. Remove from the heat.

In a large mixing bowl combine the eggs, cream, salt, and pepper. Beat well with an electric mixer or by hand with a wire whisk. Lightly mix in the spinach, the cheddar cheese, and ¾ cup of pesto (the remaining pesto can be used in salad dressings or frozen for later use).

Pour the mixture into the pie shell. Bake at 425° for 10 minutes, then reduce the heat to 300° and bake 20 to 25 minutes or until a knife inserted in the center comes out clean. Cover with buttered aluminum foil if the quiche browns too quickly.

Shrimp and Tomato Quiche
with Parmesan Cheese

6 servings

4 tablespoons butter
½ pound medium shrimp,
  shelled and roughly
  chopped
1 medium onion, diced
1 clove garlic, minced
2 large ripe tomatoes, peeled,
  seeded, and chopped
1 tablespoon dried oregano
1 tablespoon tomato paste

½ cup white wine
6 large eggs
¼ cup heavy cream
1 teaspoon salt
1 teaspoon ground black
  pepper
¾ cup grated parmesan
  cheese
1 Unbaked Pie Shell

HEAT the butter in a frying pan over low to medium heat. Sauté the shrimp until they are just opaque. Remove them with a slotted spoon, and set aside in a mixing bowl.

Melt the remaining butter in the frying pan. Add the onion and garlic. Sauté until the onion is clear, but not brown. Add the tomatoes, oregano, tomato paste, and wine. Simmer gently for about 20 minutes, until the mixture has thickened.

In a large mixing bowl beat the eggs well. Add the cream, salt, and pepper. Beat until thoroughly mixed.

Add the warm tomato mixture to the bowl containing the shrimp. Mix in the parmesan cheese until the cheese melts slightly.

Add the tomato, shrimp, and cheese mixture to the egg mixture, and blend well.

Gently pour the filling into the pie shell. Bake at 425° for 10 minutes to brown the crust, then at 300° for 20 to 25 minutes, until the custard is set and a knife inserted in the center comes out clean.

This quiche is delicious with mimosas for brunch. At lunch or dinner it goes well with Mandarin Orange, Walnut, and Papaya Salad.

Onion, Walnut, and Swiss Quiche

6 servings

3 tablespoons butter
2 large white onions, diced
2 cloves garlic, minced
¾ cup chopped walnuts
6 eggs
1¼ cups light cream

1 teaspoon salt
1 teaspoon ground black
  pepper
1 teaspoon ground nutmeg
1 cup grated swiss cheese
1 Unbaked Pie Shell

HEAT the butter in a frying pan over low to medium heat. Sauté the onions and garlic until the onions are soft and clear. Add the walnuts, and toast for about 5 minutes. Remove from the heat and set aside.

Combine the eggs, cream, salt, pepper, and nutmeg in a large mixing bowl. Beat well with an electric mixer or by hand with a wire whisk. Lightly stir the walnut and onion mixture and the swiss cheese into the egg mixture.

Pour the filling into the pie shell. Bake at 425° for 10 minutes, then reduce the heat to 300° and bake for 25 to 30 minutes, until a knife inserted in the center comes out clean. Cover the quiche with buttered aluminum foil if it browns too quickly.

The Breakfast, *drypoint etching by Anders Zorn, 1898. Short Gallery.*

Brie and Thyme Quiche

6 servings

3 tablespoons butter	1 teaspoon ground nutmeg
2 large onions, diced	1 teaspoon salt
2 cloves garlic, minced	1 teaspoon ground black
¾ pound chilled brie cheese,	pepper
rind removed, sliced very	6 eggs
thin	1¼ cups light cream
1 tablespoon dried thyme	1 Unbaked Pie Shell

HEAT the butter in a frying pan over low to medium heat. Sauté the onions and garlic until the onions are clear and soft. Reduce the heat to very low. Add the slices of brie and allow them to melt, stirring constantly. Add the thyme, nutmeg, salt, and pepper. Mix well. Keep the mixture warm over very low heat.

In a large mixing bowl, combine the eggs and cream. Beat well with an electric mixer or by hand with a wire whisk.

Spread the brie mixture over the bottom of the pie shell. Pour in the egg mixture. Mix lightly with your fingers, being careful not to damage the bottom of the pie shell.

Bake at 425° for 10 minutes, then reduce the heat to 300° and bake for 25 to 30 minutes, until a knife inserted in the center comes out clean. Cover the quiche with buttered aluminum foil if it browns too quickly.

Roquefort and Apple Quiche

6 servings

4 tablespoons butter
1 large white onion, diced
2 tart apples, such as Granny Smith, cored, peeled, and sliced
1 teaspoon ground black pepper

1 teaspoon ground nutmeg
¾ cup chilled Roquefort cheese
6 eggs
1¼ cups light cream
½ teaspoon salt
1 Unbaked Pie Shell

HEAT the butter in a frying pan over medium heat. Sauté the onion and apples until the onion is clear and soft. Remove from the heat and set aside.

In a large mixing bowl mash the pepper and nutmeg into the cheese. Gently mix in the onion and apple mixture. Set aside.

Combine the eggs, cream, and salt in a large mixing bowl. Beat well with an electric mixer or by hand with a wire whisk. Lightly stir in the apple and Roquefort mixture.

Pour the mixture into the pie shell. Bake at 425° for 10 minutes. Reduce the heat and bake at 300° for 25 to 30 minutes, until a knife inserted in the center comes out clean. If the quiche browns too quickly cover it with buttered aluminum foil.

Apple and Cheddar Quiche

6 servings

3 tablespoons butter
3 tart apples, such as Granny
  Smith, cored, peeled, and
  sliced
¼ cup brandy
6 eggs
1¼ cups light cream

1 teaspoon salt
1 teaspoon ground black
  pepper
1 teaspoon ground nutmeg
1 cup grated cheddar cheese
1 Unbaked Pie Shell

HEAT the butter in a frying pan over low to medium heat. Sauté the apples for about 3 minutes, until softened. Add the brandy, and sauté for about 5 minutes, until the alcohol dissipates. Remove from the heat and set aside.

In a large mixing bowl combine the eggs, cream, salt, pepper, and nutmeg. Beat well with an electric mixer or by hand with a wire whisk. Lightly mix in the apples and cheddar.

Pour the mixture into the pie shell. Bake at 425° for 10 minutes, then reduce the heat to 300° and bake for 25 to 30 minutes, until a knife inserted in the center comes out clean. If the quiche browns too quickly cover it with buttered aluminum foil.

Smoked Salmon Quiche with Cream Cheese

6 servings

1 cup softened cream cheese
2 tablespoons minced fresh
  dill
½ teaspoon ground cumin
1½ cups light cream
3 tablespoons butter
6 large scallions, trimmed
  and diced
1 large sweet red pepper,
  diced

4 ounces (¾ cup) smoked
  salmon, cut into small
  pieces
6 eggs
1 teaspoon salt
2 teaspoons ground black
  pepper
1 Unbaked Pie Shell

COMBINE the cream cheese, the dill, the cumin, and ¼ cup of the light cream in a large mixing bowl. Beat on low speed with an electric mixer until the dill is well distributed and the mixture is creamy.

Heat the butter in a frying pan over low to medium heat. Sauté the scallions and peppers until softened. Add the cream cheese mixture, and let it melt over very low heat.

Combine the remaining cream, eggs, salt, and pepper in a large mixing bowl. Beat well with an electric mixer or by hand with a wire whisk.

Spread the cream cheese mixture over the bottom of the pie shell. Arrange the salmon pieces on top of the cream cheese. Pour in the egg mixture. Lightly mix the filling with your fingers, being careful not to damage the bottom of the shell.

Bake the quiche at 425° for 10 minutes, then reduce the heat to 300° and bake for 25 to 30 minutes, until a knife inserted in the center comes out clean. If the quiche browns too quickly cover it with buttered aluminum foil.

Apple and Cheddar Quiche with Chicken

6 servings

1 cup white wine
¼ cup orange juice
6 tablespoons butter
1 pound boneless chicken breasts
3 tart apples, such as Granny Smith, cored, peeled, and sliced
¼ cup brandy

6 eggs
1¼ cups light cream
1 teaspoon salt
2 teaspoons ground black pepper
1 teaspoon ground nutmeg
1 cup grated cheddar cheese
1 Unbaked Pie Shell

IN A frying pan bring the wine, the orange juice, and 3 tablespoons of butter to a simmer. Poach the chicken breasts (do not boil) for about 7 minutes on each side, until the meat is cooked through. Remove from the heat, discard the liquid, and set the chicken aside to cool.

Heat the remaining butter in a frying pan over low to medium heat. Sauté the apples until they are soft. Add the brandy; sauté for another 5 minutes, or until the alcohol dissipates. Remove from the heat and set aside.

Mince the cooled chicken breasts. Add to the apples.

In a large mixing bowl combine the eggs, cream, salt, pepper, and nutmeg. Beat well with an electric mixer or by hand with a wire whisk. Lightly stir in the apple-chicken mixture and the cheddar cheese.

Pour the mixture into the pie shell. Bake at 425° for 10 minutes, then reduce the heat and bake at 300° for 25 to 30 minutes, until a knife inserted in the center comes out clean. If the quiche browns too quickly cover it with buttered aluminum foil.

Eggplant, Tomato, and Basil Quiche with Cheddar

6 servings

4 tablespoons butter
1 large onion, diced
2 cups peeled and chopped eggplant
½ cup tomato purée
¼ cup tomato paste
½ cup white wine
2 tablespoons dried basil
½ cup grated parmesan cheese

6 eggs
1¼ cups light cream
1 teaspoon salt
2 teaspoons ground black pepper
1 cup grated cheddar cheese
1 Unbaked Pie Shell

HEAT the butter in a frying pan over low to medium heat. Sauté the onion and eggplant until the onion is soft and clear. Add the tomato purée, tomato paste, wine, and basil. Simmer over very low heat for 20 minutes, or until the eggplant is well cooked and any excess liquid has evaporated. Stir in the parmesan cheese. Remove from the heat and set aside.

In a large bowl combine the eggs, cream, salt, and pepper. Beat well with an electric mixer or by hand with a wire whisk. Lightly stir in the eggplant mixture and cheddar cheese.

Pour the mixture into the pie shell. Bake at 425° for 10 minutes, then reduce the heat to 300° and bake for 25 to 30 minutes, until a knife inserted in the center comes out clean. If the quiche browns too quickly cover it with buttered aluminum foil.

LUNCHEON PIES

A page from John Singer Sargent's Spanish sketchbook. Short Gallery.

Artichoke Cheese Pie

6 servings

2 10-ounce cans artichoke
hearts in brine, drained
and chopped
2 medium onions, chopped
1 stick (¼ pound) butter
2 cloves garlic, minced
3 tablespoons all-purpose
flour
2 eggs, beaten

2 teaspoons ground nutmeg
2 teaspoons ground oregano
2 teaspoons ground black
pepper
1 cup grated swiss cheese
¼ cup grated parmesan
cheese
½ cup heavy cream
Pastry for a Double Crust Pie

BRING 6 cups of water to a boil, then remove from the heat.
Soak the artichokes in the water until it cools, about 20 minutes.
Drain the artichokes, then rinse them and drain again to remove
the brine.

Sauté the onions in the butter over medium heat until clear.
Add the garlic; sauté until the garlic is lightly cooked.

Transfer the onions and garlic to a large mixing bowl. Immediately add in the order given: the flour, the eggs, the nutmeg,
the oregano, the pepper, and both cheeses. Mix thoroughly after
each addition. Add the artichokes and the cream; mix well.

Roll out pastry for the bottom crust and lay it in the pie pan.
Spread the filling mixture over. Cover with the remaining pastry,
and crimp the edges. Bake at 350° for 45 minutes, until the crust
is golden brown.

Serve very hot with crisp greens in vinaigrette.

Ratatouille Pie

6 servings

1 stick (¼ pound) butter
1 large onion, diced
8 cloves garlic, minced
1 large green pepper, diced
1 large sweet red pepper, diced
2 stalks celery, diced
1 cup sliced mushrooms
1 small zucchini, diced
1 medium eggplant (½ pound), peeled and cut into ½-inch cubes (about 2 cups)
½ cup pitted and chopped black olives
1 cup tomato purée
¼ cup tomato paste
1 cup red wine
1 tablespoon dried basil
1 tablespoon dried oregano
1 teaspoon salt
1 teaspoon ground black pepper
2 cups washed and trimmed spinach leaves, tightly packed
½ cup grated parmesan cheese
1 Unbaked Pie Shell
1 cup herbed bread crumbs
Sour cream

HEAT 6 tablespoons of the butter in a very large frying pan over low to medium heat. Sauté the onion, garlic, peppers, and celery until the onion is soft and clear.

Add the mushrooms, zucchini, and eggplant, then sauté for 5 minutes.

Add the olives, tomato purée, tomato paste, wine, basil, oregano, salt, pepper, spinach leaves, and parmesan. Simmer for about 30 minutes, until the vegetables are tender and the excess liquid has evaporated. Remove from the heat.

Spread the mixture in the pie shell.

Heat the remaining 2 tablespoons of butter in a clean frying pan over low heat. Stir in the bread crumbs; toast lightly. Sprinkle them over the top of the pie.

Bake the pie at 350° for 30 to 40 minutes. Serve topped with sour cream.

Salmon Pie

6 servings

1 cup white wine (if using fresh salmon)	½ cup minced fresh dill
1½ pounds salmon fillets, or 1 pound canned salmon	1 teaspoon ground cumin
	1 tablespoon paprika
1 stick (¼ pound) butter	1 teaspoon ground black pepper
1 large onion, diced	
4 cloves garlic, minced	1 teaspoon salt
¼ cup all-purpose flour	½ cup heavy cream
1 cup mashed potatoes	3 eggs, separated
	1 Unbaked Pie Shell

TO PREPARE fresh salmon: Put the white wine and salmon fillets in a shallow pan over low heat. Simmer gently until the fish is just cooked through, about 5 to 10 minutes. Remove from the heat, and set aside in a large bowl. When the fish has cooled, remove the bones. To prepare canned salmon: Place the salmon and the liquid from the can in a large bowl. Remove the bones.

Heat the butter in a frying pan over low to medium heat. Sauté the onion and garlic until the onion is clear. Add the flour slowly, stirring until it dissolves into the butter. Add to the bowl containing the fish.

Add the mashed potatoes, dill, cumin, paprika, pepper, salt, cream, and egg yolks to the fish mixture. Lightly purée in a food processor, or in small batches in blender, until well mixed and smooth.

Beat the egg whites with an electric mixer or a wire whisk until stiff peaks form. Gently fold the egg whites into the fish mixture. Transfer the mixture to the unbaked pie shell.

Bake the pie at 350° for about 40 minutes, until the filling has set and a knife inserted in center comes out clean.

Serve with a sauce of 3 parts sour cream and 1 part horseradish, or with ketchup. A green salad or spiced coleslaw would be a good accompaniment.

ide Oxeyes in the meads
that gaze

Cornish Meat Pie

6 servings

2 pounds lean ground beef
2 medium carrots, diced
1 medium onion, diced
1 large potato, peeled and
  diced
3 tablespoons butter
3 tablespoons flour
1 cup Beef Stock
1 tablespoon minced garlic

4 tablespoons each of minced
  fresh basil, marjoram, and
  thyme, or 1 tablespoon
  each dried
1 teaspoon salt
1 teaspoon ground black
  pepper
Pastry for a Double-Crust Pie

IN A frying pan over moderate heat simmer the ground beef in enough water to cover. When the meat is thoroughly cooked, drain off the liquid. Transfer the meat to a large mixing bowl. Break up any lumps, and mash until the ground beef acquires a fine texture.

Boil the carrots, onion and potato until soft. Drain, reserving about ½ cup of the liquid. Add the vegetables to the meat in the mixing bowl.

In a frying pan over moderate heat, heat the butter until it froths, then subsides. Dissolve the flour into the butter. Gradually whisk in the stock, beating until smooth. Add the garlic and herbs, and simmer for 5 minutes.

Add the liquid to the beef and vegetables. The mixture should be very moist, but not runny. If it is too dry, add a little of the cooking liquid from the vegetables. Add the salt and pepper. Adjust the seasonings.

Pour the mixture into the pie shell; cover, and crimp the edges. Bake at 350° for about 45 minutes, until the crust is golden brown.

Cornish Meat Pie is very rich and garlicky. A clean-tasting green vegetable or salad would complement it well.

Opposite: Illustration from Flora's Feast *by Walter Crane. Library.*

Veal and Mushroom Pie

6 servings

1½ pounds veal cutlets, pounded thin and cut in short, narrow strips
2 cups dry sherry
8 cloves garlic, minced
2 tablespoons minced fresh oregano, or 1 tablespoon dried
2 tablespoons minced fresh basil, or 1 tablespoon dried
1 tablespoon Worcestershire sauce
6 strips bacon
2 large carrots, peeled and sliced thin lengthwise

1 large white potato, peeled and sliced in thin rounds
1 medium white onion, diced
6 tablespoons butter
¼ cup all-purpose flour
½ pound small white mushrooms, sliced thin
½ cup heavy cream
2 eggs, well beaten
1 teaspoon salt
1 teaspoon ground black pepper
Pastry for a Double-Crust Pie

MARINATE the veal pieces in the sherry, garlic, oregano, basil, and Worcestershire sauce for at least 2 hours. Drain, reserving the liquid.

In a frying pan over low to medium heat, fry the bacon until it is slightly crisp but still pliable. Set it on paper towels to drain.

Boil the carrots and potato in a pan of water until the vegetables are tender but still firm. Drain gently and set aside.

Sauté the onion in 4 tablespoons butter over low to medium heat until the onion is clear. Gradually add the flour, stirring until it dissolves. Set aside.

Heat the remaining butter in a large, clean frying pan over low to medium heat. Sauté the mushrooms for 5 minutes. Remove them with a slotted spoon, and set aside. Add the veal; sauté for 5 minutes. Add the reserved marinade; simmer for about 10 minutes, until the liquid reduces by half. Add the onion-flour mixture and the mushrooms. Let simmer for 15 to 20 minutes, stirring well to form a gravy. When the mixture is smooth, transfer it to a large bowl. Cool for ½ hour.

Add the heavy cream, eggs, salt, and pepper to the mixture. Stir well.

To assemble the pie, roll out the bottom crust and place it in the pie pan. Spread the potatoes evenly over it, and spread the veal mixture over the potatoes. Place the strips of carrot and bacon, alternating the two, on top of the veal mixture. Cover with the remaining pastry; crimp the edges and vent the top.

Bake the pie at 350° for 45 minutes, or until the crust is golden brown. Serve very hot.

Chicken and Vegetable Pie

6 servings

2 pounds boneless chicken
  breasts, diced
½ cup all-purpose flour
4 tablespoons butter
6 cloves garlic, minced
1 cup Chicken Stock
½ cup dry white wine
4 bay leaves
2 tablespoons minced fresh
  thyme, or 1 teaspoon dried
¼ cup minced fresh
  marjoram, or 1 tablespoon
  dried

2 tablespoons minced fresh
  sage, or 1 teaspoon dried
¼ cup minced fresh parsley
2 large white potatoes, peeled
  and diced
1 large white onion, diced
2 large carrots, diced
1 teaspoon salt
2 teaspoons ground black
  pepper
2 eggs, beaten
Pastry for a Double-Crust Pie

LIGHTLY dust the chicken pieces with the flour. Melt half the butter in a large frying pan over low to medium heat, and brown half the chicken pieces. Remove with a slotted spoon and set aside. Melt the remaining butter in the pan, and brown the rest of the chicken; set aside. Add the garlic to the pan; sauté lightly. Add the chicken stock, white wine, bay leaves, thyme, marjoram, sage, parsley, and chicken pieces. Simmer for 10 minutes, until the liquid thickens and the chicken is just cooked through. Transfer to a large bowl.

Boil the potatoes, onion, and carrots until the vegetables are tender but still firm. Drain. Add the vegetables to the chicken mixture, and let cool for 20 minutes.

Add the salt and pepper. Adjust the seasonings. Add the beaten eggs, being careful the mixture is not hot enough to cook them.

Roll out the pastry for the bottom crust and place it in the pie pan. Top with the chicken and vegetable mixture. Cover with the remaining pastry, crimp the edges, and vent the top. Bake at 350° for 45 minutes, until the crust is golden brown.

Spicy, marinated green beans or mushrooms are a good side dish with this pie.

Beef Pie

6 servings

2 pounds sirloin tips, sliced
  very thin
½ cup all-purpose flour
6 tablespoons butter
1 large white onion, diced
6 cloves garlic, minced
4 bay leaves
½ pound small white
  mushrooms, sliced
½ pound spinach, washed
  and trimmed
1 cup dry red wine
2 teaspoons tomato paste
½ cup Beef Stock

1 teaspoon ground allspice
1 tablespoon dried oregano
½ teaspoon grated orange
  rind
1 teaspoon salt
1 teaspoon ground black
  pepper
2 large white potatoes, peeled
  and diced
2 large carrots, diced
1 quart water
Pastry for a Double-Crust Pie
  (see recipe)

DUST the sirloin tips in the flour; set aside.

Heat 3 tablespoons of the butter in a large frying pan over low to medium heat. Sauté the onion, garlic, bay leaves, and mushrooms until the onion is clear and the mushrooms are cooked through. Add the spinach; cover. Let the spinach wilt over low heat then raise the heat slightly and sauté the spinach for about 2 to 3 minutes. Remove the mixture with a slotted spoon; transfer to a bowl.

Add 1 tablespoon butter to the pan. Brown a third of the beef pieces. Brown the rest of the beef in two more batches, using 1 tablespoon butter for each batch. Add all the beef to the pan, and add the red wine. Stir in the tomato paste; let it dissolve. Add the beef stock, allspice, oregano, orange rind, salt, and pepper. Simmer over low heat for 15 minutes. Add the onion and spinach mixture; simmer for 5 minutes more. The liquid should be very thick. Transfer the mixture to a large bowl.

Boil the potatoes and carrots in water until the vegetables are tender but still firm. Drain. Add the vegetables to the beef mixture in the bowl. Mix well.

Roll out the pastry for the bottom crust and place it in the pie pan. Top with the beef and vegetable mixture. Cover with the remaining pastry, crimp the edges, and vent the top. Bake at 350° for 45 minutes, until the crust is golden brown.

Steak and Kidney Pie

6 servings

1 pound beef kidneys
¼ cup brandy
1 pound sirloin tips, sliced
   thin
½ cup all-purpose flour
6 tablespoons butter
1 small white onion, diced
2 cloves garlic, minced
4 bay leaves
½ pound white mushrooms,
   sliced

1 large white potato, peeled
   and diced
½ cup Beef Stock
2 tablespoons Worcestershire
   sauce
1 tablespoon dried basil
1 tablespoon dried allspice
1 teaspoon salt
1 tablespoon ground black
   pepper
Pastry for a Double-Crust Pie

TRIM the fat from the kidneys. Place them in a bowl and rinse well. Set the bowl under a thin stream of running water for 15 minutes. Slice the kidneys very thin, and marinate them in the brandy for ½ hour.

Dust the sirloin tips with the flour. Set aside.

Heat 3 tablespoons butter in a frying pan over low to medium heat. Sauté the onion, garlic, bay leaves, and mushrooms until the onion is clear and the mushrooms are cooked through. Remove with a slotted spoon and transfer to a large bowl.

Boil the potato in water until the pieces are tender but still firm. Drain and set aside.

Drain the kidneys, reserving the brandy. Add the remaining butter to the frying pan, and brown the sirloin pieces. Add the onion-mushroom mixture to the pan. Add the kidneys, brandy, beef stock, Worcestershire sauce, basil, allspice, salt, and pepper. Simmer for about 15 minutes, until the meat is cooked through and the liquid has thickened.

Roll out pastry for the bottom crust and place it in the pie pan. Top with the steak and kidney mixture. Cover with the remaining pastry, crimp the edges, and vent the top. Bake at 350° for 45 minutes, until the crust is golden brown.

Smoked Scallop Pie

6 servings

1 stick (¼ pound) butter
1 small onion, diced
2 cups Fish Stock (see recipe)
½ cup white wine
¾ pound white fish, such as haddock
4 tablespoons all-purpose flour
¾ pound smoked bay scallops

1 cup mashed potatoes
3 eggs, well beaten
3 tablespoons minced fresh parsley
1 teaspoon salt
1 teaspoon ground white pepper
½ cup heavy cream
1 Unbaked Pie Shell

HEAT 4 tablespoons of the butter in a frying pan over medium heat. Sauté the onion until clear. Add the fish stock, the wine, and the fish. Simmer over low heat until the fish is opaque. Remove it from the pan and set aside. Simmer the stock until it reduces to about 1 cup. Set aside.

Immediately melt the rest of the butter in the frying pan; heat until it gets frothy, then subsides. Slowly, whisk in the flour. When the flour is all dissolved, begin slowly whisking in the fish stock mixture. Whisk until smooth, then let simmer very gently for about 5 minutes. Remove from the heat.

In a food processor or in small batches in a blender, purée half the scallops, the potato, and the fish, and the fish stock mixture.

Transfer the scallop and potato mixture to a large mixing bowl. Mix in the eggs, parsley, salt, pepper, and heavy cream. Beat with a wooden spoon for about 30 strokes. Add the remaining scallops; mix well.

Pour the mixture into the pie shell. Bake at 350° for about 40 minutes, until a knife inserted in the center comes out clean.

This pie is best topped with sour cream flavored with horseradish and accompanied by Spiced Coleslaw.

Tourtière
(French-Candian Pork Pie)

6 servings

1½ pounds ground pork
(blade or shoulder)
½ pound lead ground beef
4 bay leaves
3 cloves garlic, minced
2 large white potatoes, peeled
and diced
1 large white onion, diced

3 tablespoons all-purpose
flour
1 tablespoon ground cloves
2 teaspoons ground allspice
1 teaspoon salt
1 teaspoon ground black
pepper
Pastry for a Double-Crust Pie

GENTLY simmer the pork, beef, bay leaves, and garlic in water
to cover over low heat, until the meat is cooked through. Drain,
reserving 1 cup of the liquid. Transfer the meat to a large mixing
bowl. Mash well with a potato masher to remove lumps and
achieve a smooth consistency.

While the meat cooks, boil the potatoes and onion until they
are tender but still firm. Drain; add the vegetables to the meat
mixture.

Warm the reserved liquid from the meat in a small pan over
low heat. Whisk in the flour, allowing it to dissolve; some lumps
will remain. Strain through a fine sieve to remove lumps. Add
to the meat and potato mixture. Mix well.

Add the cloves, allspice, salt, and pepper to the mixture.

Roll out pastry for the bottom crust and place it in the pie
pan. Spread the meat and potato mixture over. Cover with the
remaining pastry, crimp the edges, and vent the top. Bake at
350° for 45 minutes, until the crust is golden brown.

This pie should be served with ketchup, baked beans and as-
sorted relishes and pickles. In my family it is traditionally served
on New Year's Day.

Ham and Ricotta Pie with Raisins

6 servings

6 tablespoons butter	1½ pounds whole-milk
¾ cup finely chopped	ricotta cheese
walnuts	2 eggs, beaten
1 small white onion, diced	1 teaspoon ground cinnamon
½ pound Virginia ham,	½ teaspoon ground cloves
sliced thin and cut into 1-	½ teaspoon ground allspice
inch squares	1 teaspoon salt
½ cup minced fresh parsley	1 teaspoon ground black
1½ cups raisins	pepper
⅓ cup Grand Marnier	1 Unbaked Pie Shell
½ cup heavy cream	

HEAT the butter in a frying pan over low to medium heat. Add the walnuts, and toast lightly. Remove them with a slotted spoon, and set aside.

Add the onion to the butter in the pan; sauté until clear. Add the ham, parsley, and raisins. Sauté for about 5 minutes. Add the flour slowly, allowing it to dissolve into the butter. Add the Grand Marnier and heavy cream; mix well. Simmer for 3 minutes, until the liquid has thickened. Remove from the heat and set aside.

In a large mixing bowl combine the ricotta cheese, eggs, cinnamon, cloves, allspice, salt, and pepper. Beat with an electric mixer, or by hand with a wire whisk, until the ingredients are blended and the mixture is smooth. Stir in the ham and raisin mixture by hand.

Sprinkle the walnuts over the bottom of the pie shell. Spread the ricotta mixture over them. Bake the pie at 350° for 30 to 35 minutes, until the filling bounces back lightly when touched and a knife inserted in the center comes out clean.

This pie is excellent for brunch. It is light and fluffy, but very rich.

Illustration from Baby's Bouquet *by Walter Crane. Library.*

Chilled Avocado Pie

6 servings

4 cloves garlic, minced
Juice of 1 lemon
3 ripe avocados, peeled
1 teaspoon salt
½ teaspoon cayenne pepper
½ teaspoon ground nutmeg
½ teaspoon ground cumin
¼ cup minced fresh cilantro
3 eggs, separated, at room
  temperature

1½ tablespoons cornstarch
1¾ cups heavy cream
½ cup orange juice
3 tablespoons unflavored
  gelatin
1 Unbaked Pie Shell
Sour cream

PURÉE in a food processor, or in small batches in a blender, the garlic, lemon juice, avocados, salt, cayenne pepper, nutmeg, cumin, and cilantro. Cover tightly and refrigerate.

Combine the egg yolks and cornstarch. Beat with a wire whisk.

Heat ¾ cup of heavy cream in a small pan over low to medium heat; do not boil. Remove the cream from the heat and add it gradually to the egg yolk mixture, stirring constantly. Transfer the mixture to a double boiler, and heat until it thickens (about 10 minutes), stirring constantly. Do not allow the water to boil. Transfer the custard to a large bowl, and let cool.

While the custard cools, heat the orange juice in a small pan until it almost boils. Remove from the heat. Stir in the gelatin very slowly, until it dissolves completely. Beat the remaining cup of cream until it is very stiff. Chill.

When the custard has cooled, mix in the gelatin and avocado purée. Chill in an ice bath until the mixture thickens, stirring constantly. Remove from the ice bath and fold in the whipped cream.

Beat the egg whites until stiff peaks form. Fold them into the avocado mixture. Chill the mixture for 1 hour.

While the filling chills, prepare the pie shell. Cover it with heavily buttered aluminum foil, and fill the cavity with dried peas or beans. Bake at 350° for 35 minutes, then remove the weights. Bake for 10 minutes more, until the pastry is flaky and golden brown. Let cool 20 minutes.

Spread the custard mixture in the pie shell. Refrigerate overnight, or at least 5 hours. If the filling browns a little on top, scrape off a thin layer with a knife. Beat the sour cream with an electric mixer or wire whisk until it becomes smooth and slightly liquified. Slice the pie with a warm knife and serve. Pour the sour cream over the slices.

The Wedding Feast at Cana *by Tintoretto, Venetian, sixteenth century. Long Gallery.*

Main Dishes, Hot and Cold

HOT MAIN DISHES

Dinner party at the home of Mr. and Mrs. John L. Gardner, Beacon Street, Boston, around 1890. Standing, Mr. Gardner; second from the right, Mrs. Gardner. Gardner Museum archives.

Veal Stew with Rosemary and Allspice

6 to 8 servings

6 cups Beef Stock
2 cups dry red wine
1 tablespoon grated orange
  peel
4 tablespoons fresh rosemary,
  or 1 tablespoon dried
1 tablespoon ground allspice
½ cup tomato paste
1 large white onion, chopped
1 large carrot, chopped
2 cloves garlic, crushed
3 bay leaves
3 pounds veal cutlets
½ cup all-purpose flour
13 small Red Bliss potatoes,
  quartered

12 small white boiling
  onions, halved
1 stick (¼ pound) unsalted
  butter
½ pound mushrooms,
  quartered
1 cup dry sherry
4 large sweet red peppers,
  sliced thin
½ pound spinach leaves,
  washed and trimmed
Salt and pepper to taste,
  about 1 teaspoon each

IN A large pot combine the beef stock, wine, orange peel, rosemary, allspice, tomato paste, onion, carrot, garlic, and bay leaves. Gently simmer for about ½ hour. Strain, discarding the solids. Set aside 2 cups of stock; transfer the rest to a large bowl.

Cut the veal into strips about ½-inch wide and 3 inches long. Set aside 3 tablespoons flour; dredge the veal strips in the rest.

In a large pot, simmer the potatoes and onions in enough water to cover them until the potatoes are almost, but not quite, cooked through. Drain; add the potatoes and onions to the bowl containing the beef stock.

In a large frying pan over medium heat, melt 2 tablespoons of the butter. Add the mushrooms and cook, stirring constantly, about 4 minutes. Add ¼ cup of the sherry; let simmer for 5 minutes, until the alcohol has evaporated and the mushrooms are cooked through. Remove the mushrooms with a slotted spoon and add them to the bowl containing the beef stock, potatoes, and onions.

Melt 2 more tablespoons of the butter in the frying pan. Add the peppers and cook for 3 or 4 minutes, then add ¼ cup of the sherry and the spinach. Let simmer about 5 minutes, until the peppers are soft and the alcohol has evaporated. Remove the peppers with a slotted spoon and add them to the beef stock mixture.

Melt the remaining butter in the frying pan. Brown the veal pieces in 2 or 3 batches over medium heat. Remove the veal with a slotted spoon, and transfer it to the bowl containing the beef stock mixture.

Add the reserved 3 tablespoons flour to the frying pan. Stir well until the flour dissolves, adding a little more butter if necessary. Add the remaining sherry and the 2 cups of reserved beef stock. Beat with a wire whisk until smooth. Strain to remove lumps, and add to the beef stock mixture.

Transfer the contents of the bowl to a large stockpot. Simmer over low heat for about 1 hour, until the sauce thickens. Add the salt and pepper. Adjust the seasonings.

Serve in large bowls with warm caraway rye bread and unsalted butter.

Chicken Casserole with Mushrooms and Bacon in Cream Sauce

6 servings

1 cup Chicken Stock
½ cup dry white wine
1 tablespoon dried thyme
Stems from 1 small bunch
  parsley
8 pieces medium-crisp bacon,
  drained well
12 miniature carrots, peeled
  and trimmed, or 5
  medium-sized carrots,
  peeled, trimmed, and sliced
  into 3-inch sticks
8 small new potatoes, peeled
  and cut into 1-inch pieces

9 small white boiling onions,
  halved
4 tablespoons butter
½ pound mushrooms
1 cup sherry
6 chicken breasts, boned,
  skinned, and halved
1 cup all-purpose flour
2½ cups heavy cream
Salt and pepper to taste,
  about 1 teaspoon each

IN A saucepan over low to moderate heat, simmer the chicken stock, wine, thyme, parsley stems, and 2 pieces of the bacon for 30 minutes. Remove from the heat; set aside.

In a saucepan boil the carrots, potatoes, and onions in water to cover until the vegetables are tender but still firm. Drain and set aside.

Wipe the mushrooms clean with a damp paper towel. Trim the stems, and slice the mushrooms in half.

In a large frying pan over medium heat, melt 1 tablespoon of the butter. Add the mushrooms and cook for 2 to 3 minutes, stirring constantly. Then add the sherry and cook for 5 minutes more. Remove the mushrooms from the pan with a slotted spoon, and set them aside.

Dredge the chicken breast in the flour. In 3 or 4 batches, using a portion of the remaining butter for each batch, brown the chicken breast in the frying pan over medium heat, about 45 seconds on each side. (The chicken need not cook through;

if browned too long it will toughen.) Set the browned chicken aside.

Stir the chicken stock into the frying pan, whisking until smooth. Add the heavy cream, and let simmer for 10 minutes, until the liquid thickens. Strain, and discard any lumps or solids. Add salt and pepper to taste. Adjust the seasonings.

Break the remaining bacon into 1-inch pieces.

In a large shallow baking dish, arrange the chicken pieces, vegetables, and bacon. Pour in the cream sauce; it should almost cover the chicken. Cover the dish, and bake at 325° for about 30 minutes, until the chicken is cooked through. Serve very hot.

Hot Sliced Green Beans in Vinaigrette are a good complement to this dish.

Marinated Chicken Breasts
in Curried Cream Sauce

6 servings

½ cup orange juice
1 cup dry white wine
¼ cup vegetable oil
½ cup minced fresh parsley
2 cloves garlic, minced
3 tablespoons peeled and
  grated gingerroot
6 boneless chicken breasts, fat
  trimmed

1 cup Chicken Stock
2 large sweet red peppers,
  diced
1 tablespoon curry powder
1 teaspoon ground cloves
1 teaspoon salt
1 teaspoon ground black
  pepper
2½ cups heavy cream

COMBINE the orange juice, wine, oil, parsley, garlic, and ginger. Marinate the chicken in the mixture for at least 1 hour.

Remove the breasts from the marinade. Heat the marinade and the chicken stock in a shallow pan wide enough to hold all the chicken breasts. Allow the mixture to simmer 5 minutes. Add the chicken breasts and peppers; the liquid should not cover the breasts. Simmer gently, taking care the liquid does not boil, about 15 minutes, until the chicken is just cooked through. Do not overcook. Remove the chicken and set aside.

Add the curry powder, cloves, salt, and pepper. Add the heavy cream; simmer for 20 minutes. Remove from the heat.

Arrange the chicken in a shallow baking dish. Pour the cream sauce over the chicken; cover. Bake at 350° for 20 minutes. Serve hot.

Roast Turkey Breast Stuffed with Pesto in Tomato Butter

6 to 8 servings

2 large (1½-pound) turkey breasts, halved

1 tablespoon butter, softened
½ cup white wine

FOR THE PESTO:
2 cups basil leaves, freshly washed and tightly packed
4 cloves garlic, minced
½ cup pine nuts
½ cup grated parmesan cheese

1 teaspoon salt
1 teaspoon ground black pepper
½ cup olive oil

FOR THE TOMATO BUTTER:
8 shallots, chopped
1 teaspoon tomato paste
¼ cup tomato purée
¼ cup white wine
¼ cup white vinegar
2 tablespoons minced fresh parsley

1 teaspoon ground white pepper
½ teaspoon salt
2 sticks (½ pound) very cold unsalted butter, cut into small pieces

PURÉE the pesto ingredients in a food processor, or in small batches in a blender, until very smooth. Set aside.

With a very sharp boning knife, make incisions about 1 inch apart on the inner, rough side of the turkey breast halves. Do not cut all the way through; leave at least a ¼-inch thickness. As you cut, flatten the breasts until they have a uniform thickness of about 2 inches. Rub the cut side with the softened butter.

Lay the turkey breasts out flat, smooth side down. Spread the pesto mixture evenly over the cut side of the breasts, in a layer no more than ⅛-inch thick. Roll up the breasts lengthwise, and

Opposite: Mrs. Gardner in Yellow and Gold *by James McNeill Whistler, 1886. Veronese Room.*

tie securely with string. Trim the ragged edges from each roll.

Arrange the breasts in a 9-by-12-inch baking dish. Pour the wine into the bottom of the dish. Cover, and bake at 350° for 45 minutes, until the turkey is just cooked through. Be careful not to overcook it. Let cool for 5 minutes before slicing.

Thirty minutes before serving the turkey, place the shallots, tomato paste, tomato purée, wine, and vinegar in a saucepan over low to medium heat. Simmer for 10 to 20 minutes, until the liquid reduces by half. Strain through a fine sieve, and return to a clean pan. Add the parsley, salt, and pepper; simmer for 1 minute. Over very low heat, add the butter 1 piece at a time, beating briskly with a wire whisk until each piece dissolves. (If the butter starts to clarify—that is, separate into fat, solids, and water—turn off the heat. If necessary, immerse the pan in very cold water and beat the contents vigorously with a wire whisk. Beat in all the butter pieces. Reheat briefly and gently if necessary, beating constantly.)

Remove the string from the turkey breasts. Slice each roll crosswise into rounds, with the pesto showing in a spiral. Pool the warm tomato butter on plates, and place the hot turkey pieces in the butter. Serve immediately.

This dish goes well with hot, buttered noodles and Mushroom, Pea Pod, and Red Pepper Salad.

Baby Lamb Chops with Cilantro Butter

6 servings

18 baby lamb rib chops,
   about 3 ounces each
3 tablespoons butter

3 tablespoons sherry
1 teaspoon white pepper

FOR THE CILANTRO BUTTER:

8 shallots, chopped
½ cup white wine
¼ cup white vinegar
½ cup minced fresh cilantro
   (also called chinese parsley
   or coriander)

½ teaspoon salt
1 teaspoon ground white
   pepper
2 sticks (½ pound) very cold
   unsalted butter, cut into
   very small pieces

TRIM most of the fat from the lamb chops, leaving a layer of about ⅛ inch. Make small incisions across the remaining fat layer to prevent curling. Dot the lamb chops with the butter; sprinkle them with the sherry and the pepper.

To make the cilantro butter, simmer the shallots, wine, and vinegar in a medium-sized saucepan over low to medium heat for 10 to 20 minutes, until the liquid reduces by half. Strain through a fine sieve, and return the liquid to a clean pan. Add the cilantro, salt, and pepper. Simmer for 5 minutes over very low heat. Add the butter 1 piece at a time, beating with a wire whisk until each piece dissolves. (If the butter starts to clarify—that is, separate into fat, solids, and water—turn off the heat. If necessary, immerse the pan in very cold water and beat the contents vigorously with a wire whisk. Beat in all the butter pieces. Reheat briefly and gently if necessary, beating constantly.)

Immediately place the lamb chops under a very hot broiler. Broil about 2½ minutes on each side. The cooked chops should be pink inside.

Pool the warm butter on plates, and place 3 lambchops on each. Serve immediately.

This dish goes well with hot Tomato, Corn, and Lima Bean Succotash.

Fillet of Sole with Julienned Carrots in Creamy Dill Sauce

6 servings

6 ½ pound sole fillets
2 tablespoons butter
18 medium, firm white
    mushrooms, sliced thin
½ cup dry sherry

½ cup minced fresh dill
3 medium carrots, finely
    julienned
1½ cups heavy cream
2 teaspoons white pepper

PLACE the sole fillets on a buttered broiling pan. Preheat the broiler.

Melt the butter in a large frying pan over low to medium heat. Sauté the mushrooms for 1 minute. Add the sherry, dill, and carrots; cover and simmer about 5 minutes. Add the cream and pepper. Simmer about 7 minutes more, uncovered, until the liquid has reduced by a third and the carrots are slightly crisp. Adjust the seasonings, and keep warm.

Place the sole fillets under the hot broiler. Broil for 3 to 7 minutes on one side only, until just cooked through. The fish will flake when done. Serve immediately with the cream sauce.

Opposite: stoneware Greybeard jug from Frechen, Germany, seventeenth century.

Bluefish Fillets Marinated in Rice Wine with Spicy Tomato Sauce

6 servings

1 cup sweet rice cooking
    wine (mirin)
Juice from 1 lemon
½ cup minced fresh parsley
2 large green peppers, seeded
    and chopped fine
2 jalapeño peppers, minced
6 cloves garlic, minced
¼ cup vegetable oil

6½ pounds bluefish fillets
6 large ripe tomatoes
1 tablespoon butter
1 large white onion, minced
2 bay leaves
2 tablespoons tomato paste
2 teaspoons ground cumin
1 tablespoon salt

COMBINE the rice wine, lemon juice, parsley, green peppers, jalapeño peppers, garlic, and oil. Mix well. Marinate the bluefish fillets in the mixture for at least 2 hours.

Drain the fillets, reserving the marinade. Arrange the fillets in a buttered baking dish. Cover and bake at 350° for 25 to 30 minutes, until the fish flakes. Check it often toward the end of the baking period so it does not overcook.

Plunge the tomatoes into boiling water, then into ice water. Remove the skins from the tomatoes; seed and chop them.

Heat the butter in a frying pan over low to medium heat. Add the reserved marinade, onion, bay leaves, tomatoes, tomato paste, cumin, and salt. Simmer for about 45 minutes over low heat, until the vegetables are tender. Adjust the seasonings.

Serve the bluefish fillets topped with the sauce.

Poached Salmon Steaks
with Papaya Butter

6 servings

1½ cups dry white wine
2 tablespoons butter

6 bay leaves
6 ½-pounds salmon steaks

FOR THE PAPAYA BUTTER:
5 shallots, chopped
1 cup dry white wine
½ cup white cider vinegar
1 ripe papaya, peeled, seeded, and chopped fine
¼ cup minced fresh parsley

1 teaspoon ground white pepper
½ teaspoon salt
2½ sticks (10 ounces) very cold unsalted butter, cut into small pieces

IN A large frying pan simmer the 1½ cups wine, the butter, and the bay leaves over low heat until the liquid reduces by a third. Arrange the salmon steaks in the pan. Cover; poach for 10 minutes. Do not allow the liquid to boil.

While the salmon is poaching, simmer the shallots, wine, vinegar, and papaya in a medium saucepan over low heat for about 15 minutes, until the liquid reduces by half. Purée in a food processor, or in small batches in a blender, and pour the liquid into a clean saucepan. Add the parsley, pepper, and salt; simmer for 5 minutes.

Reduce the heat to very low. Add the butter pieces one at a time, beating with a wire whisk until each piece dissolves. (If the butter starts to clarify—that is, separate into fat, solids, and water—turn off the heat. If necessary, immerse the pan in very cold water, and beat the contents vigorously with the whisk. Beat all the butter pieces. Reheat briefly and gently, if necessary, whisking constantly.)

Pool the butter in the plates. Place one steak on each plate, and serve.

Peppers Stuffed with Rice, Pine Nuts, and Currants

8 servings

16 medium green bell
   peppers, well shaped
1½ cups white rice
1½ cups water
¾ cup currants
3 tablespoons butter
¾ cup finely diced celery
2 cups finely diced onion
1 tablespoon minced garlic
¾ cup pine nuts
4 cups tomato purée

½ cup orange juice
1½ cups dry white wine
¼ cup minced parsley
1 sweet red pepper, diced
1 tablespoon ground
   cinnamon
1 teaspoon salt
1 teaspoon ground black
   pepper
¼ teaspoon ground cloves

SLICE 1 inch off the tops of the peppers, reserving the caps. Remove the seeds, and arrange the peppers upright in a deep baking dish with a cover.

Place the rice and water in a medium saucepan. Simmer very gently until all the water is absorbed but the rice is still firm, about 20 minutes. Transfer the rice to a large mixing bowl. Add the currants.

In a medium frying pan over moderate heat, melt the butter. Sauté the celery, 1 cup of the onion, the garlic, and the pine nuts until the onion is clear. Add this mixture to the rice and currants.

In a large saucepan simmer the tomatoes, the orange juice, 1 cup of the wine, the parsley, the red pepper, the cinnamon, the salt, the pepper, the cloves, and the remaining onion. Let cook very gently for 45 minutes.

Purée the tomato sauce in a food processor, or in small batches in a blender. Add enough to the rice mixture to moisten it thoroughly without making it soupy.

Spoon the mixture into the green peppers. Replace the tops of the peppers. Add the remaining ½ cup of wine to the baking dish, and cover. Bake at 350° for about 45 minutes. The peppers should be thoroughly cooked, but still firm.

Reheat the remaining tomato sauce. Pool the sauce on the plates, and place the peppers on top. Serve two peppers per person as a main dish, or one per person as a side dish.

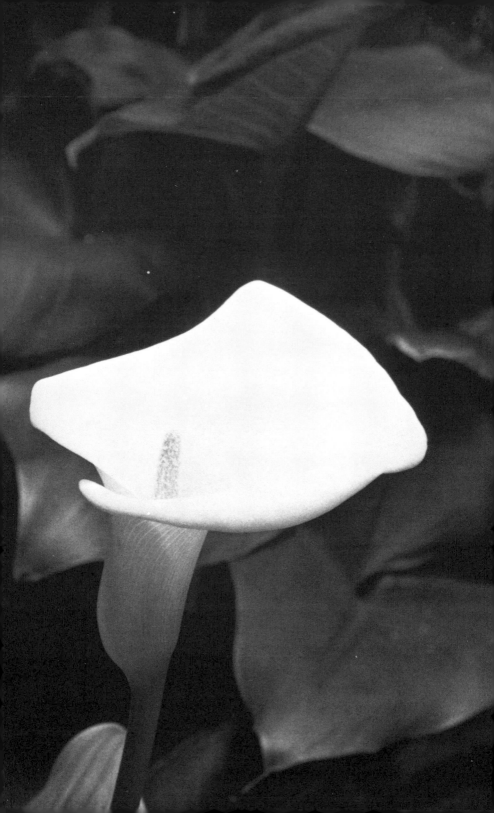

Cabbage Stuffed with Ground Beef and Apples

6 servings

2 large white cabbages	1 large onion, minced
2 quarts plus 2 cups water	2 teaspoons ground cloves
2 tablespoons butter	½ teaspoon ground nutmeg
4 large tart apples, such as Granny Smith, sliced	½ teaspoon ground allspice
1 pound ground beef	1½ cups cooked white rice
	1 cup dry white wine

CORE the cabbages and remove their tough outer leaves. Place 1 cabbage upright in a large pot. Pour in 1 quart water, and bring to a boil. Steam the cabbage for 15 to 20 minutes. Remove from the heat and drain; let the cabbage cool. Repeat this process for the second cabbage. When both cabbages have cooled break them apart, setting aside 18 good, whole leaves.

Heat the butter in frying pan over low to medium heat. Sauté the apples for about 2 minutes, until they are soft but not mushy. Remove them with a slotted spoon, and set them aside. Add the ground beef, onion, and remaining 2 cups water to the pan. Simmer for about 15 minutes, till the onion is tender. Drain. Transfer the meat mixture to a large bowl. Add the cloves, nutmeg, allspice, and rice. Mix well.

One by one, lay the cabbage leaves out flat. Place 3 or 4 slices of apple and about 3 tablespoons beef mixture on each leaf. Fold in the edges and roll the leaves up, beginning at the core end. Secure the rolls with toothpicks. Place them in a baking dish with a cover.

When all the leaves are rolled, pour the wine into the baking dish. Cover, and bake at 350° for 30 to 40 minutes.

Opposite: a calla lily in the Court.

Linguine and Vegetables in Walnut Sauce

6 servings

2 large carrots, peeled and sliced in thin rounds	1 cup puréed walnuts
2 large parsnips, peeled and sliced in thin rounds	6 shallots, minced
½ pound small white mushrooms, trimmed	1 cup dry white wine
	1 tablespoon paprika
	1 teaspoon ground white pepper
3 cups broccoli florets	1 teaspoon salt
3 tablespoons butter	2 cups heavy cream
½ cup minced fresh parsley	1½–2 pounds fresh linguine

COOK the carrots and parsnips in 2 quarts boiling water until the vegetables are tender, about 5 minutes. Add the mushrooms; boil 3 minutes, until they are cooked through. Add the broccoli; cook for 2 minutes more. Drain. Keep the vegetables warm in a covered dish.

Heat the butter in a large frying pan over low to medium heat. Sauté the parsley, walnuts, and shallots until the walnuts are lightly toasted and the shallots are clear. Add the wine, paprika, pepper, and salt. Simmer for 10 minutes over low heat. Add the cream, and simmer for 5 minutes more, stirring constantly.

Boil the linguine in 3 quarts water for 3 minutes. Drain well. Toss the linguine with enough walnut sauce to moisten. Serve the vegetables and remaining walnut sauce separately.

COLD MAIN DISHES

Paul Verlaine, French poet, in a Parisian café. Gardner Museum archives.

Scallops and Shrimp with Saffron Fettucine in Cream Sauce

6 to 8 servings

1½ pounds fresh saffron fettucine or plain fettucine
¾ cup light cooking oil, such as sunflower seed oil
4 cloves garlic, peeled and bruised
1 pound medium shrimp, peeled
1 pound bay scallops
2 large sweet red peppers, peeled and julienned

½ cup dry sherry
½ teaspoon powdered saffron
¼ teaspoon ground cumin
1½ cups heavy cream
¼ cup minced fresh cilantro (also called chinese parsley or coriander)
¼ cup chopped scallions
Salt and pepper to taste, about 1 teaspoon each

BRING 3 quarts water to a boil in a large pot. Add the fettucine; boil for 3 minutes until cooked, but still firm. Drain; rinse well with cool water. Transfer the fettucine to a large bowl. Toss it lightly with ¼ cup of the oil.

Heat the remaining oil in a large frying pan over moderate heat. Add the garlic cloves; sauté them until they release a strong aroma, but do not let them brown. Remove them with a slotted spoon.

Add the shrimp to the frying pan. Sauté until they are just opaque, stirring constantly. Remove the shrimp with a slotted spoon, and set aside in a large bowl to cool. Sauté the scallops the same way, and add them to the bowl containing the shrimp. The shrimp and scallops will release their juices as they cool.

Add the peppers to the frying pan. Sauté for 1 minute, then add the sherry. Sauté for another 3 or 4 minutes, until the alcohol dissipates. Remove the peppers with a slotted spoon, and add them to the shrimp and scallops.

Add the saffron, cumin, and heavy cream to the frying pan. Stir well to mix, then simmer 5 minutes. Remove from the heat, and add to the peppers, scallops, and shrimp. Let the mixture cool for about ½ hour.

Add the pepper, shrimp, and scallop mixture to the fettucine. Stir in the cilantro, scallions, salt, and pepper.

Serve slightly warm with warm french bread and unsalted butter, and fresh greens in vinaigrette. Or serve chilled with a tropical fruit cup.

Smoked Mussels and Spinach Linguine in Cream Sauce

6 to 8 servings

3 cups heavy cream
¼ cup dry sherry
½ cup minced fresh
marjoram
½ cup minced fresh oregano
1 teaspoon ground white
pepper

1 teaspoon salt
1½–2 pounds fresh spinach
linguine
2 pounds smoked mussels (or
substitute 2 pounds cooked
oysters)

SIMMER the cream, sherry, marjoram, oregano, pepper, and salt for ½ hour over low heat, until the liquid reduces by a third. Remove from the heat.

While the cream sauce simmers, boil the linguine in 3 quarts water for 3 minutes. Drain. Rinse with cold water.

Combine the mussels, linguine, and cream sauce. Chill for at least 2 hours. Adjust the seasonings and serve.

Smoked Salmon and Linguine in Ginger Cream Sauce

6 to 8 servings

3 cups heavy cream
½ cup cream sherry
½ cup minced fresh parsley
3 tablespoons peeled and grated gingerroot
3 cloves garlic, minced
1 teaspoon ground white pepper
1 teaspoon salt
1½–2 pounds fresh linguine
1 pound smoked salmon, cut in 1-inch strips

SIMMER the cream, sherry, parsley, ginger, garlic, pepper, and salt for ½ hour over low to medium heat until the liquid reduces by a third.

While the cream sauce simmers, boil the linguine in 3 quarts water for 3 minutes. Drain. Rinse with cold water.

Combine the salmon, linguine, and cream sauce. Chill at least 2 hours. Adjust the seasonings and serve.

Marinated Smoked Salmon
with Potato-Cucumber Salad
and Red Peppers in Sherry

6 to 8 servings

FOR THE SALMON:
1 cup olive oil
Juice of 1 lemon
1 tablespoon ground black
  pepper

½ cup capers
1 tablespoon dry sherry
1 pound smoked salmon,
  sliced thin

FOR THE PEPPERS:
½ cup olive oil
4 large red bell peppers,
  seeded and sliced thin,
  lengthwise

¾ cup dry sherry

FOR THE POTATO-CUCUMBER SALAD:
6 Red Bliss potatoes,
  quartered
3 medium cucumbers, peeled,
  quartered lengthwise,
  seeded, and sliced
1½ cups sour cream

¼ cup prepared horseradish
¼ cup minced fresh dill
1 tablespoon ground black
  pepper
1 teaspoon salt

FOR GARNISH:
Black olives
Trimmed scallions

Hard-boiled eggs

BLEND the olive oil, lemon juice, pepper, capers, and sherry.
Add the salmon, and marinate for at least 1 hour.

Heat the oil in a frying pan. Sauté the peppers for 5 minutes.
Add ½ cup sherry; simmer for 10 minutes. Remove from the
heat; add the remaining sherry. Chill.

Opposite: Wine Glass, *etching by James McNeill*
Whistler, 1859. Short Gallery.

Boil the potatoes until tender but not mushy. Drain, and transfer to a large bowl. Add the cucumbers. Chill.

Combine the sour cream, horseradish, dill, pepper, and salt. Add to the potato-cucumber mixture. Adjust the seasonings.

Arrange the salmon, the peppers, and the potato-cucumber salad on individual plates. Garnish with the olives, scallions, and hard-boiled eggs.

Salade Niçoise with Fresh Tuna and Sun-dried Tomatoes

6 servings

6 small new potatoes, peeled and cut into 1-inch cubes
¾ pound young, tender green beans, trimmed
Whole inner leaves of 1 head romaine lettuce
1¼ pounds fresh tuna steaks, sliced thin

1 cup sun-dried tomatoes packed in oil, cut into thin strips
½ pound niçoise olives, or any small black olives
6 scallions, trimmed and sliced lengthwise

FOR THE DRESSING:
1½ cups olive oil
Juice of 1 lemon
1 tablespoon Dijon mustard
½ cup balsamic vinegar
1 teaspoon salt

1 teaspoon ground black pepper
¼ cup minced fresh basil
¼ cup minced fresh parsley

BOIL the potatoes until just tender, but not mushy. Drain, and rinse gently with cold water. Let the potatoes dry in a strainer. Chill.

Bring 6 cups of water to a boil. Drop in the green beans; boil 4 minutes, until they are bright green. Immediately transfer them to an ice-water bath. When the beans have chilled drain them, pat them dry, and refrigerate them.

Vigorously whisk together the dressing ingredients. The dressing should be smooth and thick.

Arrange the potatoes, the beans, and the other salad ingredients attractively on a platter or on individual plates. Serve the dressing on the side.

Shrimp and Beef Salad
with Tropical Fruit

6 servings

1½ cups vegetable oil
1½ pounds medium shrimp, peeled
1 pound beef sirloin, cut into thin strips
4 kiwis, peeled, quartered, and sliced
3 ripe papayas, seeded, peeled, and sliced lengthwise

½ ripe pineapple, cut into chunks
Whole inner leaves of 1 head romaine lettuce
6 scallions, trimmed and sliced lengthwise
1 pound seedless green grapes

FOR THE DRESSING:
Juice of 5 limes
1½ cups olive oil
1 teaspoon salt
1 teaspoon ground black pepper

2 teaspoons Dijon mustard
¼ cup minced fresh tarragon

HEAT ¾ cup oil in a frying pan over low to medium heat. Sauté the shrimp until just opaque. Transfer to a small bowl.

Add the remaining oil to the pan. Sauté the beef pieces. Transfer to a separate bowl.

Combine the kiwi, papaya, and pineapple in a third bowl.

Combine all the dressing ingredients, and whisk until smooth. Reserve half the dressing. Divide the rest among the bowls containing the fruit, beef, and shrimp, and stir to coat all ingredients. Place all 3 bowls in the refrigerator to chill.

Arrange the lettuce leaves, fruit, beef, and shrimp attractively on a large platter. Garnish with the scallions and grapes. Serve the remaining dressing on the side.

Opposite: Blue Worcester-ware pitcher, nineteenth century. Yellow Room.

Chilled Veal Salad
with Spinach and Mushrooms
in Fresh Tomato and Garlic Sauce

6 servings

1 cup vegetable oil
½ pound white mushrooms, sliced
1½ cups dry sherry
6 sweet red peppers, seeded and sliced

1½ pounds fresh spinach, trimmed
2½ pounds veal cutlets, cut into strips
1 head romaine lettuce

FOR THE TOMATO SAUCE:

6 large ripe tomatoes
8 cloves garlic, minced
1 cup orange juice
1 cup dry white wine
½ cup tomato paste

1 teaspoon salt
2 teaspoons ground black pepper
¼ cup minced fresh parsley
¼ cup minced fresh basil

HEAT ½ cup oil in a frying pan over low to medium heat. Sauté the mushrooms for 5 minutes. Add ½ cup dry sherry; simmer 5 minutes. Remove the mushrooms with a slotted spoon, and transfer them to a large bowl.

Add the peppers to the pan. Sauté them for 5 minutes, then add another ½ cup sherry and the spinach leaves. Cover and simmer 5 minutes, until the spinach leaves are barely wilted. Remove the peppers and spinach with a slotted spoon; add them to the mushrooms.

Pour the remaining ½ cup of oil into the pan. Sauté the veal pieces in 2 or 3 batches until they are done. Add the remaining ½ cup of sherry to the pan; simmer 5 minutes. Transfer the entire contents of the pan to the bowl containing the mushrooms, peppers, and spinach. Mix well. Chill.

Plunge the tomatoes into boiling water for 3 minutes, then briefly into ice water, and remove their skins. Squeeze out most of the seeds, and rinse the tomatoes well to remove the rest. Combine the tomatoes, garlic, orange juice, wine, and tomato paste. Simmer over low heat for 45 minutes, then purée in a food processor or in small batches in a blender. Strain the sauce through a fine sieve. Stir in the salt, pepper, parsley, and basil. Chill.

Arrange the lettuce leaves on a large platter. Mound the veal, mushroom, and pepper mixture in the center. Drizzle half the tomato sauce over, and serve the rest on the side.

Veal and Tomato Mousse

12 servings

2 cups dry white wine
2 pounds veal cutlets
1 large white onion, chopped
3 cloves garlic, minced
2 teaspoons salt
2 teaspoons ground black
    pepper
4 large ripe tomatoes

½ cup tomato paste
4 eggs, separated
2 tablespoons cornstarch
3 cups heavy cream
½ cup orange juice
2 tablespoons unflavored
    gelatin

FOR THE PESTO:
2 cups fresh basil leaves,
    firmly packed
½ cup pine nuts
¾ cup olive oil
½ cup grated parmesan
    cheese

3 cloves garlic, minced
1 teaspoon salt
1 teaspoon ground black
    pepper

HEAT 1 cup of the wine in a frying pan over low to medium heat. Add the veal, half the onion, half the garlic, 1 teaspoon salt, and 1 teaspoon pepper. Simmer until the veal is cooked through. Remove from the heat, and drain. Purée in a food processor, or in small batches in a blender, until smooth. Set aside to cool.

Plunge the tomatoes into boiling water for 3 minutes, then briefly into ice water. Remove the skins, squeeze out most of the seeds, and rinse to remove the rest.

Heat the remaining wine in the frying pan. Add the tomatoes, the tomato paste, and the remaining onion, garlic, salt, and pepper. Simmer for 25 minutes. Remove from the heat. Purée in a food processor, or in small batches in a blender, until smooth. Strain through a sieve. Set aside to cool.

Beat together the egg yolks and cornstarch. Heat 1½ cups heavy cream in a small saucepan, taking care that it does not boil. When hot, remove the cream from the heat and add it gradually to the egg yolks, stirring constantly. Transfer the mixture to a double boiler set over medium heat. Stirring constantly, allow the mixture to thicken about 10 minutes. Remove from the heat, and let cool.

Heat the orange juice in a small saucepan, taking care that it does not boil. Remove from the heat, and slowly stir in the gelatin so that it completely dissolves. Stir the orange juice into the egg mixture. Divide the mixture between 2 mixing bowls. Add the veal purée to 1 bowl, the tomato purée to the other. Place the bowls in ice baths, and stir until the mixtures thicken. Remove them from the ice baths, and set aside.

Beat the remaining 1½ cups heavy cream until stiff peaks form. Fold half into the veal mixture, and half into the tomato mixture.

Beat the egg whites until stiff peaks form. Fold half into the veal mixture, and half into the tomato mixture. Chill the mixtures 1 hour.

Purée all the pesto ingredients in a food processor, or in small batches in a blender until smooth.

Spread the veal mixture in an oiled 8-inch square casserole with a smooth inside surface. Place the casserole in an ice bath for 30 minutes. Remove it from the ice bath, and gently pour the pesto over the veal in a thin layer. Gently spread the tomato mixture on top of pesto. Cover the casserole with oiled plastic wrap, and chill for at least 6 hours.

To unmold, dip the casserole briefly in hot water, and turn the mousse out onto a platter. Slice with a warm knife.

Serve with a salad of New Potatoes in Tarragon Mayonnaise.

Chicken and Pea Pod Salad
with Fettuccine and Cilantro

6 servings

1½ cups vegetable oil
2½ pounds boned and
skinned chicken breasts,
diced
1 cup orange juice
1 cup dry white wine
6 red bell peppers, seeded
and sliced lengthwise

1 cup dry sherry
1 pound snow pea pods,
trimmed
10 ounces fresh red pepper
fettuccine or plain
fettuccine

FOR THE VINAIGRETTE:
¾ cup vegetable oil
⅓ cup red wine vinegar
2 shallots, minced
1 teaspoon Dijon mustard
1 teaspoon salt

1 teaspoon ground black
pepper
¾ cup minced cilantro (also
called chinese parsley or
coriander)

HEAT ½ cup oil in a frying pan over low to medium heat. Brown the chicken pieces lightly. Add the orange juice and wine, and simmer for about 7 minutes, until the chicken is just cooked through. Do not let the liquid boil, and do not let the chicken overcook, or it will be tough. Drain, and set the chicken aside to cool at room temperature.

Heat the remaining oil in a clean pan over low to medium heat. Sauté the peppers until tender but still firm, about 10 minutes. Add the sherry and pea pods; let simmer about 10 more minutes, until the alcohol has dissipated. Transfer the entire contents of the pan to a large bowl. Let cool slightly at room temperature, then add the chicken.

To make the vinaigrette, combine all ingredients in a large bowl and beat well with a wire whisk, or mix them till smooth

Opposite: nasturtiums in the Court.

in a food processor or blender. Add the vinaigrette to the still warm chicken and vegetable mixture.

Cook the fettuccine in 3 quarts boiling water about 2 minutes. Drain, rinse with cold water, and shake out excess water. Add the fettuccine to the other ingredients. Let the salad chill in the refrigerator at least 1 hour. Adjust the seasonings and serve.

Chicken and Pesto with Tortellini

6 servings

¾ cup vegetable oil
2 pounds boned and skinned chicken breasts, diced
1 cup orange juice
1 cup dry white wine
3 small zucchini, quartered lengthwise and sliced in wedges

10 ounces fresh cheese tortellini
18 cherry tomatoes, halved
Black olives
Grated parmesan cheese

FOR THE PESTO:

½ cup olive oil
2 cups fresh basil leaves, firmly packed
½ cup pine nuts
4 cloves garlic, minced

½ cup grated parmesan cheese
1 teaspoon salt
1 teaspoon ground black pepper

HEAT ½ cup oil in a large frying pan over low to medium heat. Brown the chicken pieces lightly. Add the orange juice and wine, and simmer—do not boil—until the chicken is cooked through, about 10 minutes. Do not overcook, or the chicken will toughen. Drain, and transfer the chicken to a large bowl to cool at room temperature.

Heat the remaining ¼ cup oil in a clean frying pan over low to medium heat. Sauté the zucchini pieces until lightly done, about 5 minutes; they should still be crisp. Add them to the chicken.

Cook the tortellini in 3 quarts boiling water for about 5 minutes. Drain, rinse with cool water, shake out the excess water, and add the tortellini to the chicken.

To make the pesto, purée the ingredients in a food processor, or in small batches in a blender, until smooth. Combine the pesto with the chicken mixture, adding a little more oil if necessary.

Let the salad chill in the refrigerator at least 1 hour. Adjust the seasonings. Serve garnished with the halved cherry tomatoes and the olives. Serve the grated parmesan cheese on the side.

Chicken, Pear, and Grape Salad
with Lemon-Garlic Mayonnaise

6 servings

½ cup vegetable oil
2½ pounds boned and
    skinned chicken breasts,
    diced
1 cup orange juice
1 cup dry white wine
4 ripe anjou pears, sliced
    lengthwise and sprinkled
    with lemon juice

3 cups black olives
1 large canteloupe, seeded,
    skinned, and cut into 1-
    inch cubes
1 pound seedless green
    grapes
Whole inner leaves of 1 head
    romaine lettuce
1 cup chopped walnuts

FOR THE MAYONNAISE:
2 egg yolks
1 egg white
3 cloves garlic, minced
¼ cup minced fresh parsley
¼ cup lemon juice

1 teaspoon salt
1 teaspoon ground black
    pepper
1 tablespoon Dijon mustard
2 cups vegetable oil

HEAT the oil in a frying pan over low to medium heat. Brown
the chicken pieces lightly. Add the orange juice and wine, and
simmer—do not boil—about 7 minutes, until the chicken is just
cooked through. Do not overcook, or the chicken will toughen.
Drain, and set the chicken aside to cool in a large bowl.

When the chicken is cool, add the pears, olives, canteloupe,
and grapes.

To make the mayonnaise, combine all ingredients except the
oil in a food processor or blender, and purée 2 minutes. Slowly
pour in the oil, allowing it to emulsify with the eggs. Adjust the
seasonings. Add the mayonnaise to the chicken and fruit.

Arrange the lettuce leaves on a large platter or on individual
plates. Arrange the salad on the lettuce leaves, and garnish with
the walnuts.

*Third-century Roman sarcophagus with satyrs and maenads gathering grapes. West
Cloister.*

Chicken and Avocado Salad
with Tangerines, Papayas, and Walnuts

6 servings

½ cup vegetable oil
2 pounds boned and skinned chicken breasts, diced
1 cup orange juice
1 cup white wine
4 tangerines, peeled and sectioned
4 ripe papayas, peeled, seeded, and sliced lengthwise

4 avocados, peeled, seeded, sliced, and sprinkled with lemon juice
Whole inner leaves of 1 head romaine lettuce
1½ cups chopped walnuts
6 scallions, chopped

FOR THE DRESSING:
1½ cups vegetable oil
½ cup tarragon vinegar
¼ cup minced fresh tarragon
1 teaspoon salt

1 teaspoon ground black pepper
1 teaspoon Dijon mustard

HEAT the oil in a frying pan over low to medium heat. Brown the chicken pieces lightly. Add the orange juice and wine, and simmer—do not boil—7 minutes, until the chicken is just cooked through. Do not overcook, or the chicken will be tough. Drain, and set the chicken aside in a large bowl to cool.

To make the dressing, combine all ingredients in a large bowl. Beat well with a wire whisk, or briefly whir in a blender at low speed.

Add the tangerine, papaya, and avocado to the chicken. Add half the dressing, and mix lightly.

Arrange the lettuce leaves on a large platter or on individual plates. Arrange the chicken mixture over the lettuce, and garnish with the walnuts and scallions. Serve the remaining dressing on the side.

Chilled Baked Tomatoes
Stuffed with Ratatouille and Pesto

6 servings

15 large ripe tomatoes
1 cup white wine
¾ cup vegetable oil
1 large white onion, roughly chopped
8 cloves garlic, minced
2 large green bell peppers, seeded and roughly chopped
2 stalks celery, diced
1 cup sliced mushrooms
1 medium eggplant (about ¾ pound), cut into 1-inch cubes

2 small zucchini, quartered lengthwise and sliced in wedges
½ cup chopped black olives
1 cup dry red wine
¼ cup tomato paste
¼ cup minced fresh parsley
1 teaspoon salt
1 teaspoon fresh-ground black pepper

FOR THE PESTO:

2 cups fresh basil leaves, firmly packed
½ cup pine nuts
½ cup freshly grated parmesan cheese
4 cloves garlic, minced

1 teaspoon salt
1 teaspoon ground black pepper
1 cup olive oil
¼ cup lemon juice

REMOVE the core and seeds from 3 tomatoes. Chop the tomatoes and set aside.

For the remaining tomatoes, cut a hole 1 inch in diameter around each core. Remove the core, and scrape out the seeds with a spoon. Rub the inside of the tomato with 1 teaspoon of the vegetable oil. Place all the tomatoes in a large baking dish with a cover, and pour in the white wine. Cover; bake at 350° for 30 to 35 minutes, until the tomatoes are cooked but still hold their shape. Remove them from the pan, and set them aside to cool.

Heat the remaining vegetable oil in a large frying pan over low to medium heat. Sauté the onion, garlic, peppers and celery until the onion is clear and soft. Add the mushrooms, eggplant, zucchini, olives, chopped tomatoes, red wine, tomato paste, parsley, salt, and pepper. Mix well. Simmer over low heat, stirring often, for about 30 minutes, until the vegetables are tender. Add a little water if necessary during cooking. Remove the ratatouille from the heat, and set aside to cool.

To make the pesto, combine all ingredients in a food processor or blender; purée until smooth. The mixture should have the consistency of heavy cream. Add more oil or lemon juice if necessary.

When the ratatouille has cooled, mix in the pesto gradually, adding enough to suit your taste. Spoon the mixture into the tomato shells, and chill well. Serve very cold with any remaining pesto on the side.

Zucchini Stuffed with Rice, Ground Lamb, and Tomatoes

6 servings

12 small zucchini
¼ cup vegetable oil
3 cloves garlic, minced
1 cup dry white wine
1½ pounds ground lamb
1 large onion, diced
1 quart plus 2 cups water
2 cups tomato purée
3 large ripe tomatoes, seeded
  and chopped

3 bay leaves
1 tablespoon dried oregano
1 teaspoon salt
1 teaspoon ground black
  pepper
½ teaspoon ground
  cinnamon
2 cups cooked white rice

SLICE each zucchini in half lengthwise. Drop the halves into 1 quart boiling water, a few at a time, and boil about 3 minutes. Drain well and cool slightly. Scrape out the seeds with a spoon. Combine the oil with the minced garlic, and rub the mixture over the zucchini halves. Arrange them in a shallow baking dish. Pour in the white wine. Cover, and bake at 350° about 20 minutes, until the zucchini halves are tender all the way through but still hold their shape. Set them aside to cool.

Simmer the ground lamb and onion in 2 cups water until the meat is cooked. Pour off the water, along with grease that has risen. Drain well. Mash the lamb by hand or in a food processor or blender until it is smooth, but not mushy. Return the meat to the pan.

Add to the meat the tomato purée, chopped tomatoes, bay leaves, oregano, salt, pepper, and cinnamon. Simmer over very low heat for 20 minutes. Remove to a large bowl.

Mix in the rice, and let cool. Adjust the seasonings. Divide the mixture evenly among the zucchini shells. Chill well before serving.

Overleaf: T. A. Nash's Fruit Shop, *etching by James McNeill Whistler, mid-1880s. Short Gallery.*

Side Dishes and Salads

COLD SIDE DISHES

View of the Court from the West Cloister.

Rich Vinaigrette

Serves 8 to 12

⅓ cup minced fresh parsley
1 egg
1 tablespoon Dijon mustard
¼ cup grated parmesan
  cheese
1 teaspoon salt

1 teaspoon ground black
  pepper
1½ cups vegetable oil
¼ cup red wine vinegar
⅓ cup minced fresh basil or
  dill
2 cloves garlic, minced

COMBINE all the ingredients in a large bowl. Beat with a wire whisk until thickened. (Do not use a food processor, as it would turn the dressing into mayonnaise.)

This dressing goes well with any tossed green salad or chilled vegetables. It is a favorite at the Café, where customers often ask for the recipe.

Chilled Rice in Raspberry Vinaigrette

6 to 8 servings

2 cups white rice
2½ cups water
1 teaspoon ground white
  pepper
¼ cup raspberry vinegar

1 cup vegetable oil
1 teaspoon ground nutmeg
¼ cup minced fresh parsley
½ cup minced scallion tops
4 large navel oranges

IN A covered saucepan, simmer the rice in the water until the water is absorbed and the rice is tender, but still firm. Add more water during cooking if necessary. Transfer the cooked rice to a bowl. Add the salt, pepper, vinegar, oil, and nutmeg. Let cool.

With a very sharp knife, carefully remove the peels and pith from the oranges, being careful not to cut into the fruit. Remove the membrane from each section, and squeeze the juice from the leftover membrane. Add the orange sections and juice to the rice mixture. Stir in the parsley and scallions.

Let the rice marinate 1 hour in the refrigerator. Adjust the seasonings and serve.

New Potatoes in Tarragon Mayonnaise

6 to 8 servings

8 medium red potatoes, cut
  into 1-inch cubes
Juice from one lemon
¼ cup vegetable oil
2 teaspoons salt

2 teaspoons ground black
  pepper
1 large onion, diced
3 stalks celery, diced
2 hard-boiled eggs, sliced

FOR THE MAYONNAISE:

3 eggs, separated
1 cup minced fresh tarragon

1 tablespoon Dijon mustard
2 cups vegetable oil

BOIL the potatoes until they are just cooked through; be careful
not to overcook them. Drain, and transfer the potatoes to a large
bowl. Add the lemon juice, oil, salt, pepper, onions, and celery.

To make the mayonnaise, combine 3 egg yolks, 1 egg white,
the tarragon, and the mustard in a food processor or blender.
Beat at least 1 minute. While the machine is running, slowly
pour in the oil, allowing it to emulsify with the eggs. (If the
mixture separates, remove it from the machine. Place an additional egg yolk and 1 teaspoon mustard in the machine; beat 1
minute; and slowly pour in the separated mixture until you
achieve the desired consistency.)

Add the mayonnaise to the potato mixture. Adjust the seasonings. Decorate with the hard-boiled eggs.

Corn and Kidney Bean Salad
with Fresh Basil

6 to 8 servings

1 pound cooked kidney beans
1 pound (4 cups) corn
2 large green bell peppers,
   seeded and chopped fine
4 large cloves garlic, minced

¾ cup minced fresh basil
3 tablespoons lemon juice
¾ cup vegetable oil
Salt and pepper to taste,
   about 2 teaspoons each

COMBINE all ingredients in a large mixing bowl. Let them marinate for at least 1 hour. The longer the salad marinates, the better it will taste.

This green, red, and yellow salad makes a very attractive side dish. The basil gives it a fresh, cool taste, but the salad is rich and hearty enough to be a meal in itself on a hot day.

Apple-Carrot Salad
with Walnut Vinaigrette

6 to 8 servings

6 large, firm Red Delicious
    apples, cored and sliced

3 large carrots, grated
3 stalks celery, diced

FOR THE VINAIGRETTE:
½ cup walnuts
1 cup vegetable oil
¼ cup red wine vinegar
⅛ cup lemon juice

1 teaspoon salt
1 teaspoon ground black
    pepper
1 teaspoon ground nutmeg

TO MAKE the vinaigrette, purée all ingredients in a food processor, or in small batches in a blender, until smooth.

In a large bowl, combine the apples, carrots, celery, and walnut vinaigrette. Adjust the seasonings and serve.

Rice Salad with Sweet Red Peppers, Shallots, and Spinach

6 to 8 servings

2 cups white rice
2½ cups water
¼ cup red wine vinegar
¼ cup lemon juice
1 cup vegetable oil
2 medium sweet red peppers, seeded and sliced into thin strips
1 cup dry sherry

3 cups washed and trimmed spinach leaves, firmly packed
5 shallots, minced
¼ cup minced fresh parsley
1 teaspoon salt
1 teaspoon ground black pepper

SIMMER the rice in the water until it is tender but still firm. Add more water during cooking if necessary. Transfer the cooked rice to a large bowl. Add the vinegar and lemon juice.

Heat the oil in a frying pan over low to medium heat. Sauté the peppers about 5 minutes. Add the sherry; let simmer 10 minutes, until the alcohol dissipates. Add the spinach leaves; allow them to just wilt. Transfer the contents of the frying pan to the bowl containing the rice.

Stir the shallots, parsley, salt, and pepper into the rice. Let the salad marinate in the refrigerator at least 1 hour. Adjust the seasonings and serve.

Opposite: The Vinegar Tasters, *a seventeenth-century Japanese screen, Kano School. Second Floor Passage.*

Mushroom, Pea Pod, and Red Pepper Salad

6 to 8 servings

1 cup vegetable oil

1 pound white mushrooms, sliced

3 large sweet red peppers, seeded and sliced lengthwise

1 cup dry sherry

1 pound snow pea pods, trimmed

¼ cup red wine vinegar

¼ cup minced fresh tarragon, or 1 tablespoon dried

1 teaspoon salt

1 tablespoon ground black pepper

HEAT the oil in a large frying pan with a cover over low to medium heat. Sauté the mushrooms and peppers 3 to 5 minutes, until softened. Add the sherry. Cover, and simmer 5 minutes. Add the pea pods; uncover, and simmer 5 minutes more. Transfer the vegetables to a bowl.

Add the vinegar, tarragon, salt, and pepper. Chill 1 hour. Adjust the seasonings and serve.

Mandarin Orange, Walnut, and Papaya Salad

6 to 8 servings

2 cups canned mandarin
 orange sections
½ cup raspberry vinegar
¾ cup vegetable oil
1 teaspoon Dijon mustard
1 teaspoon salt
1 teaspoon ground black
 pepper

1 head romaine lettuce,
 washed, chilled, and torn
1 cup plain croutons
1 large ripe papaya, peeled,
 seeded, and sliced
 lengthwise
1 cup chopped walnuts
¾ cup chopped scallions

MARINATE the oranges in ¼ cup raspberry vinegar at least 1 hour.

In a small bowl combine the vegetable oil, the remaining raspberry vinegar, the mustard, the salt, and the pepper. Beat well with a wire whisk. Pour the dressing into a cruet.

Distribute the lettuce, croutons, orange sections, papaya, walnuts, and scallions among individual bowls, or combine in a large serving bowl. Serve the dressing on the side.

Spiced Coleslaw

6 to 8 servings

4 cups finely grated red
  cabbage
6 shallots, chopped fine
1 cup golden raisins
¼ cup red wine vinegar
¾ cup vegetable oil
1 tablespoon poppy seeds
1 tablespoon celery seeds

1 teaspoon peeled and grated
  gingerroot
1 teaspoon Dijon mustard
½ teaspoon ground coriander
1 teaspoon ground black
  pepper
1 teaspoon salt

COMBINE all ingredients. Let the salad marinate in the refrigerator at least 2 hours. Adjust the seasonings and serve.

Opposite: Bread cage, or "cooler," from eighteenth-century France. Dutch Room.

Baked Sweet Potato Purée

6 to 8 servings

6 medium sweet potatoes, peeled and sliced
2 teaspoons butter
3 eggs, beaten
½ cup heavy cream
1 teaspoon ground nutmeg
½ teaspoon ground cinnamon
¼ teaspoon ground cloves
1 teaspoon salt
1 teaspoon ground black pepper
Flour

BOIL the sweet potatoes until very soft. Drain. Purée them in a food processor, or in small batches in a blender, until very smooth. Transfer them to a bowl.

Mix 1½ teaspoons of the butter into the hot sweet potato purée, allowing it to melt. Beat in the eggs, cream, nutmeg, cinnamon, cloves, salt and pepper.

Use the remaining butter to grease a 9-inch pie plate. Dust the plate with flour. Transfer the purée to the pie plate. Bake at 350° for 30 minutes, or until a knife inserted in the center comes out clean. Cut into wedges and serve.

Stuffed Mushrooms

6 to 8 servings

24 large, firm white mushrooms with stems, plus 10 small mushrooms with stems
4 tablespoons unsalted butter
6 cloves garlic, minced
¼ cup minced fresh parsley
½ cup sherry
⅓ cup unseasoned bread crumbs
1½ cups fresh crabmeat
¼ cup grated parmesan cheese
1 teaspoon salt
1 teaspoon ground black pepper
½ cup white wine

WIPE the mushrooms clean with a damp paper towel. Carefully remove the stems from the large mushrooms; set the caps aside. Mince the small mushrooms and the stems from the large mushrooms. Set aside.

Melt the butter in a frying pan over low to medium heat. Sauté the garlic and parsley briefly, about 1 minute. Add the chopped mushrooms; sauté about 3 minutes. Add the sherry; simmer 5 minutes, until the alcohol evaporates. Transfer the mushroom mixture to a large bowl.

While the mixture is still hot, add the bread crumbs; mix well. Add the crabmeat, parmesan cheese, salt, and pepper. Adjust the seasonings.

Divide the stuffing mixture evenly among the reserved mushroom caps; the stuffing should mound slightly. Arrange the mushroom caps in a shallow 9-by-12-inch baking dish with a cover. Pour the wine carefully into the bottom of the dish; it should cover the bottom half of the mushroom caps. Cover, and bake at 350° for 25 minutes. Uncover, and bake 10 minutes more to brown the tops of the mushrooms. Serve hot.

Ratatouille with Fresh Basil and Parmesan Cheese

6 to 8 servings

½ cup vegetable oil or olive oil

1 large white onion, roughly chopped

8 cloves garlic, minced

2 large green bell peppers, seeded and roughly chopped

2 stalks celery, diced

1 cup sliced mushrooms

1 medium eggplant (about ½ pound), cut into 1-inch cubes

2 small zucchini, sliced

½ cup chopped black olives

3 large tomatoes, seeded and chopped

1 cup dry red wine

¼ cup tomato paste

1 cup minced fresh basil

¼ cup minced fresh parsley

2 cups washed and trimmed spinach leaves, firmly packed

1 teaspoon salt

1 teaspoon ground black pepper

½ cup grated parmesan cheese

HEAT the oil in a large frying pan over low to medium heat. Sauté the onion, garlic, pepper, and celery until the onion is clear and soft.

Add the eggplant, zucchini, olives, tomatoes, red wine, and tomato paste. Mix well. Simmer uncovered over low heat, stirring often, about 30 minutes, until the vegetables are tender but not mushy. Add ½ cup water if necessary.

Add the basil, parsley, and spinach. Simmer until the spinach just wilts; it should remain bright green. Remove from the heat. Add the salt and pepper, and adjust the seasonings.

Serve hot or cold, topped with the parmesan cheese.

Tomato, Corn, and Lima Bean Succotash

6 to 8 servings

4 tablespoons butter
1 medium white onion, diced
3 cloves garlic, minced
¼ cup minced fresh parsley
2 bay leaves
4 large ripe tomatoes, peeled, seeded, and chopped
1 teaspoon tomato paste

1 cup white wine
1 cup Chicken Stock
8 ounces (3 cups) corn
8 ounces (3 cups) cooked lima beans
2 teaspoons salt
1 teaspoon ground black pepper

HEAT the butter in a large frying pan over low to medium heat. Sauté the onions, garlic, parsley, and bay leaves until the onion is clear and soft.

Add the tomatoes, tomato paste, chicken stock, and wine. Simmer uncovered over low heat for 15 minutes. Add the corn, lima beans, salt, and pepper. Simmer uncovered until the corn and lima beans are heated through and the liquid has reduced by half.

Hot Green Beans in Vinaigrette

6 to 8 servings

1 pound fresh green beans,
    trimmed
1 cup vegetable oil
¼ cup red wine vinegar
½ teaspoon Dijon mustard
1 clove garlic, minced

1 teaspoon dried tarragon
1 teaspoon grated orange
    rind
1 teaspoon salt
1 teaspoon pepper

FIFTEEN minutes before serving time, bring 2 quarts of water to a boil. Add the green beans. Reduce the heat and simmer for 3 to 5 minutes, until the beans are bright green and lightly cooked. Drain, and set aside.

Whisk together the oil, vinegar, mustard, tarragon, orange rind, salt, and pepper to make the vinaigrette. Transfer to a saucepan. Add the green beans, and bring to a simmer over very low heat. Serve immediately.

INDEX

A

Apple(s)
cabbage stuffed with ground
beef and, 97
-carrot salad, 131
and cheddar quiche, 56
and cheddar quiche with
chicken, 58
onion soup with cheese and,
18
and Roquefort quiche, 55
Artichoke cheese pie, 61
Avocado
and chicken salad, 120
pie, chilled, 76–77

B

Barley vegetable soup, 13
Bean(s)
black bean soup, 22
green, in vinaigrette, 142
kidney, and corn salad,
130
lima, in succotash, 141
white bean soup, 21
Beef
Cornish meat pie, 65
ground, cabbage stuffed with,
97
pies, 65, 69, 71
and shrimp salad, 108
steak and kidney pie, 71
stock, 6
Bisque, smoked scallop, 42
Bluefish fillets marinated in rice
wine, 92
Butters
cilantro, 89
papaya, 93
tomato, 87–88

C

Cabbage
spiced coleslaw, 136
stuffed, with ground beef and
apples, 97
Carrot(s)
-apple salad, 131
julienned, with fillet of sole,
90
soup, gingered cream of, 33
Casserole, chicken, with
mushrooms and bacon,
83–84. *See also* Main dishes,
hot
Celery, spiced pear soup with,
28
Cheese
apple and cheddar quiche, 56
apple and cheddar quiche with
chicken, 58
artichoke cheese pie, 61
brie and thyme quiche, 54
eggplant, tomato, and basil
quiche with cheddar, 59
ham and ricotta pie, 74
onion, walnut, and swiss
quiche, 52
onion soup with apples and,
18
ratatouille with basil and
parmesan, 140
Roquefort and apple quiche,
55
shrimp and tomato quiche
with parmesan, 51
smoked salmon quiche with
cream cheese, 57
spinach, cheddar, and pesto
quiche, 50
Chicken
apple and cheddar quiche
with, 58

L

Lamb
  chops, baby, with cilantro
    butter, 89
  ground, zucchini stuffed with,
    123
Lentil-tomato soup, 14
Linguine
  smoked salmon and, 103
  spinach, smoked mussels, and,
    102
  and vegetables in walnut
    sauce, 98
Luncheon pies, 60–78
  artichoke cheese, 61
  beef, 69
  chicken and vegetable, 68
  chilled avocado, 76–77
  Cornish meat, 65
  ham and ricotta with raisins,
    74
  ratatouille, 62
  salmon, 63
  smoked scallop, 72
  steak and kidney, 71
  tourtière (French-Canadian
    pork pie), 73
  veal and mushroom, 66–67

M

Main dishes
  cold, 99–124
  hot, 80–98
Mayonnaise
  lemon-garlic, 118
  tarragon, 129
Melon
  puréed watermelon with
    chilled peach soup, 30
  and strawberry soup, chilled,
    29
Minestrone, 16
Mousse, veal and tomato,
  112–13

Mushroom(s)
  chicken casserole with bacon
    and, 83–84
  chilled veal salad with spinach
    and, 110–11
  pea pod and red pepper salad
    with, 134
  soup, cream of, 37
  stuffed, 139
  and veal pie, 66–67
  vegetable soup with ham and,
    8
Mussels, smoked, with spinach
  linguine, 102

N

Nectarine soup, chilled, 32

O

Onion
  quiche, with walnuts and
    swiss, 52
  soup, with apples and cheese,
    18

P

Pasta
  chicken and pea pod salad
    with fettucine, 115–16
  chicken and pesto with
    tortellini, 117
  linguine and vegetables in
    walnut sauce, 98
  scallop chowder with, 24
  scallops and shrimp with
    saffron fettucine in cream
    sauce, 100–101
  smoked mussels and spinach
    linguine, 102
  smoked salmon and linguine
    in ginger cream sauce, 103

soup, with sun-dried
tomatoes, 9–10
soup, with tortellini, 39
stock, 3
succotash, 141
See also Salads, side dish;
names of vegetables
Vinaigrette dressing, 115
hot green beans in, 142
raspberry, 128
rich, 127
walnut, 131

W

Watermelon, puréed, chilled
peach soup with, 30

Z

Zucchini
soup, cream of, 43
stuffed with rice, ground
lamb, and tomatoes, 123

For your convenience:
have a copy of *The Gardner Museum Cafe*
Cookbook **sent to a friend or relative**

This cookbook may be purchased at the sales desk of
The Isabella Stewart Gardner Museum, 280 The
Fenway, Boston, Massachusetts 02115. You may also
order it by mail. Please make checks payable to the
publisher, The Harvard Common Press, and send
orders to:

The Harvard Common Press
535 Albany Street
Boston, Massachusetts 02118

- -

Please send ____ cookbooks @ $10.95 plus $3.00 postage
and handling per book.

to _____
NAME

at _____
ADDRESS

_____
CITY   STATE   ZIP

Massachusetts residents add 5% sales tax.

- -

Please send ____ cookbooks @ $10.95 plus $3.00 postage
and handling per book.

to _____
NAME

at _____
ADDRESS

_____
CITY   STATE   ZIP

Massachusetts residents add 5% sales tax.

- -

- -

Please send _____ cookbooks @ $10.95 plus $3.00 postage and handling per book.

to _____
NAME

at _____
ADDRESS

_____
CITY   STATE   ZIP

Massachusetts residents add 5% sales tax.

- -

Please send _____ cookbooks @ $10.95 plus $3.00 postage and handling per book.

to _____
NAME

at _____
ADDRESS

_____
CITY   STATE   ZIP

Massachusetts residents add 5% sales tax.

- -

Please send _____ cookbooks @ $10.95 plus $3.00 postage and handling per book.

to _____
NAME

at _____
ADDRESS

_____
CITY   STATE   ZIP

Massachusetts residents add 5% sales tax.

- -